STUDENTS HELPING STUDENTS

HAVE NO
CAREER FEAR

**Prentice
Hall Press**

A Berkley Book
Published by the Penguin Group
Penguin Group (USA) Inc.
375 Hudson Street, New York, New York 10014, USA
Penguin Group (Canada), 10 Alcorn Avenue, Toronto, Ontario M4V 3B2, Canada
(a division of Pearson Penguin Canada Inc.)
Penguin Books Ltd., 80 Strand, London WC2R 0RL, England
Penguin Group Ireland, 25 St. Stephen's Green, Dublin 2, Ireland
(a division of Penguin Books Ltd.)
Penguin Group (Australia), 250 Camberwell Road, Camberwell, Victoria 3124, Australia
(a division of Pearson Australia Group Pty. Ltd.)
Penguin Books India Pvt. Ltd., 11 Community Centre, Panchsheel Park, New Delhi—
110 017, India
Penguin Group (NZ), cnr. Airborne and Rosedale Roads, Albany, Auckland 1310,
New Zealand
(a division of Pearson New Zealand Ltd.)
Penguin Books (South Africa) (Pty.) Ltd., 24 Sturdee Avenue, Rosebank, Johannesburg 2196,
South Africa
Penguin Books Ltd., Registered Offices: 80 Strand, London WC2R 0RL, England

Copyright © 2005 by Natavi Guides, Inc.
Text design by Tiffany Estreicher
Cover design by Liz Sheehan

PRINTING HISTORY
Prentice Hall Press trade paperback edition / April 2005

ISBN: 0-7352-0394-6

This book has been cataloged by the Library of Congress

PRINTED IN THE UNITED STATES OF AMERICA

10 9 8 7 6 5 4 3 2

Praise for the **Stud**... **guides:**

"These are the kinds of guides a guidance counselor might love, with a mentor's nurturing tone." —*The New York Times*

"What sets this how-to apart from the others is its tone (think *Seinfeld*), its honest treatment of the challenges recent graduates face in today's market and its focus on succeeding once you get your foot in the door." —*Publishers Weekly*

"Quite different from the usual impenetrable books on the subject written by experts who haven't been in college since 'groovy, man' was, well, groovy . . . This book reminds me of the mantra, 'Each one, teach one.'" —*The Washington Post*

"One of the best qualities of the excellent Students Helping Students® series is the authors' sure sense of college students today [and its] practical, easy-to-absorb bits of advice that can immediately be put into practice . . . [goes] way beyond predictable problems and solutions to offer a full array of possible challenges and useful strategies for solving them." —*Booklist*

"A helpful map to have in your glove compartment–sized dorm room." —*Reading Eagle* (Reading, PA)

"The writing style and tone . . . is wonderful and couldn't be pulled off by someone my age. It's clear that the authors are peer to the reader, which really helps their credibility. I love the slang, the humor, and the way the book is organized. Overall, I love it!"
—Julie Jansen, author of *I Don't Know What I Want, but I Know It's Not This: A Step-by-Step Guide to Finding Gratifying Work*

"The fact that it has been prepared by students or recent students has a certain comforting appeal." —*Kliatt*

"A clear and concise guide ... excellent addition."

No doubt you've been bombarded with "expert" advice from your parents, professors, and countless advisors. It's time you got advice you can really use—from fellow students who've been where you're headed.

All Students Helping Students® books are written and edited by top students and recent grads from colleges and universities across the United States. You'll find no preachy or condescending advice here—just stuff to help you succeed in tackling your academic, social, and professional challenges.

A Note from the Founders of Students Helping Students®

Dear Reader,

Welcome to Students Helping Students®!

Before you dive headfirst into reading this book, we wanted to take a moment to share with you where Students Helping Students® came from and where we're headed.

It was only a few years ago that we graduated from college, having made enough mistakes to fill a *War and Peace*–sized novel, learned more and different things than we expected going in, and made some tough decisions—often without having enough advice to help us out. As we thought about our college experiences, we realized that some of the best and most practical advice we ever got came from our classmates and recent grads. And that's how the idea for Students Helping Students® books was born.

Our vision for Students Helping Students® is simple: Allow high school and college students to learn from fellow students who can share brutally honest and practical advice based on their own experiences. We've designed our books to be brief and to the point—we've been there and know that students don't have a minute to waste. They are extremely practical, easy to read, and inexpensive, so they don't empty your wallet.

As with all firsts, we're bound to do some things wrong, and if you have reactions or ideas to share with us, we can't wait to hear them. Visit www.StudentsHelpingStudents.com to submit your comments online.

Thanks for giving us a shot!

—Nataly and Avi
Creators of Students Helping Students®

Contents

About the Editors

Ben Cohen-Leadholm graduated from Wesleyan University in 1999 with a B.A. in European Literature. Soon after, he tossed his belongings into a van and headed for San Francisco. Little did he know that five (yes, five) dot-com layoffs were awaiting him in the beautiful Bay Area. Let's just say he became very familiar with severance packages and filing for unemployment. Seeking work that he deemed more socially meaningful, Ben returned to the East Coast to do grant writing and business development for a national nonprofit in Boston. Ben is now in Ghana, where he is sweating profusely, contracting malaria, and doing community-based business development in the capital, Accra.

Ari Gerzon-Kessler graduated from Wesleyan University in 1999 with a degree in African American Studies. He had a number of passions but no clear sense of how they would translate into an actual job. Which is why he up and moved to Mexico. A lifelong love for writing and learning about other cultures led Ari to Guadalajara, where he became a newspaper editor and reporter, as well as the radio host of a bilingual news program. Following a year of fajitas and 'ritas, Ari returned to his home state of Colorado, where he labored for a year as a telecommuting literary researcher. The isolation of this Internet-based job motivated Ari to find a more meaningful, interactive field of work. Teaching was a natural fit. Ari taught high school Spanish for a year and has spent the past two years as a bilingual third-grade teacher in Longmont, Colorado.

Rachel Skerritt received her B.A. from the University of Pennsylvania in 1998, with an English major and an African American Studies minor. The following year, she earned a Masters in Education, also from Penn. She then began working as an English teacher at her old high school, Boston Latin. For the next four years, she worked her tush off, grading hundreds of papers each week. Rachel is also the author of *Truth Be Told*, a college romance novel loosely based on her experience as an undergrad. Anxious to complete her second novel and eager to pursue an interest in screenwriting, she has taken a full year off from her teaching job to explore this creative venture.

Read This First

Why this book?

You're a smart, college-educated cookie, so why the heck do you need to read a book about getting a job after college? Well, you don't have to, but we think it might help. The economy might be getting out of its slump, but the job market for recent college grads is as competitive and tough as ever. You'll need every resource you can get your hands on to help you land that dream job and ace it once you get there, and we suggest that you add this book to your arsenal.

Sure, there are tons of great career-advice books out there, and they'll help you with everything from putting together your résumé to impressing the pants off your interviewers. (In fact, there's a whole section at the end of this book devoted to the many useful job-related resources out there.) But we searched and searched and couldn't find a book that focused on the many difficult and specific issues that young and bright recent college grads like you and us face once we enter the career maze. So we decided to write one.

We've tried to make this book as comprehensive and as unboring as possible. We've also worked hard to include tips and advice on not only finding a job but also excelling once you're there, as well as what to do when you're thinking of leaving (or in the unfortunate case that you get the dreaded pink slip). Getting a job is just the first step, and as we've learned, sometimes painfully, it's what comes after that step that's a big challenge. To share our experiences and lessons learned with you, we cover all aspects of navigating the early stages of your career, such as: narrowing down your many interests and figuring out a career direction, researching prospective employers, becoming a master at networking, acing your interviews and securing a great gig, excelling in your position, dealing effectively with your impossible boss, and much, much more.

We also know that having a job in the "real world" is a lot different from living in the self-contained bubble called college, so you'll find helpful hints on money matters and lifestyle adjustments.

Why us?

We know what you're thinking: "What makes these fools experts?" Well, not much, except that we've been through the gruel of a postcollege job world and lived to tell you about it. We've ripped our hair out trying to make our inexperience appear as experience on our résumés, learned to pretend to be expert networkers, survived our share of interviews, been hired and been fired, worked with bosses you can only dream about and bosses who'd make your blood boil, tried to get our colleagues to take us seriously despite the fact that we look like we're fifteen, and more.

But we know that we're just three people, and while we've been through a lot, we've not seen it all. Which is why we searched this great nation to find hundreds of other people who've been where you are and where you want to be. Their experiences and advice make up the bulk of this book—we're true believers in letting you learn from other people who've been through what you're facing. And to make sure that what the many recent grads share with you is not totally off the mark, we've asked a few experienced professionals and career counselors to pitch in with their suggestions.

We've tried to squeeze hundreds of experiences and pieces of advice into as concise of a book as possible, without leaving out any important stuff. We know you're busy, but we also know that if we had the benefit of some of this information before we jumped into the postcollege career world, we might've avoided more than a few mishaps.

Thanks for giving us a chance, and let's get started.
—Ben, Ari, and Rachel

STUDENTS HELPING STUDENTS

HAVE NO
CAREER FEAR

Ahh!

(or finding a job and a career)

"So, what are you going to do after graduation?" Ugh! If you hear your parents or second cousins twice removed ask this question once more, your ears will surely pop. We know and we wish that we could include a mute device in this book to help you out. But we figured that although the endless questioning by relatives who stick their collective nose into your business is annoying, you're probably asking yourself the same exact question—"What *am* I going to do after graduation?"

Some of you may know exactly what career path you want to pursue, and you've been researching potential jobs for years. For most of the soon-to-be or recent college grads, that's not the case. More likely, you're interested in a few things, not sure what type of job you might want, and wondering if you could pay the rent with the job that you do get.

Totally understandable. So, to help you navigate through your interests and figure out what jobs to pursue, we've put together some advice in the following sections.

- Quasi-Disclaimer
- Passion Fruit
- The Spanish Self-Inquisition
- Monica Lewinsky Was Right
- Will Work for Nothin'
- Be Promiscuous, Sort of
- You're Not Alone

Quasi-Disclaimer

Figuring out what career path to pursue after college and finding a job that fits within that path are no easy tasks. Not only do you want to find a job that's interesting, but it has to somehow pay the rent, and in this ever-competitive job environment you have to find a way to stand out from a crowd of high-achieving recent college grads and experienced professionals to get the job you want.

Don't despair. You'll figure out something you want to do, and you *will* find a job. It may not be your ideal dream job (heck, it probably won't be), and after taking it you might realize that you don't actually like what you're doing. But that's completely okay. Your first or second or third job after college is just the beginning of your career, and you'll have every opportunity to make your next gig a much more satisfying one. Remember that patience pays off, surprises abound, and every career path usually contains some curves and detours. Melissa, a career coach, says:

> We don't need to know what our life work will be when we finish college. We simply need to take interest in the threads that weave throughout our life. Over time, all the different pieces will begin to form into a cohesive whole.
>
> Developmentally, in our twenties it's not even realistic to know precisely what we want to do. It's simply our job to make the next right choice. Something unique and precious is forming.

Realizing that not all jobs are perfect, that many jobs get better over time, and that certain jobs may offer an exceptional learning experience over good pay is important. Lilia, a recent graduate and music producer, explains, "Keep in mind, your first job is never quite what you're looking for. It's meant to be a stepping stone and for you to acquire experience."

Passion Fruit

Will you absolutely, positively love your first job after college? Probably not. But you should try to find a job that interests you in some way or has something to do with things that you care about. Work takes up so much of our days that it would be a shame to be stuck in a job that makes you utterly bored and unhappy.

Which brings us to a good starting point for your job search—figuring out what it is that you're interested in. For some, this is pretty easy. If you've been writing articles from age five and you devour ten newspapers a day, go forth and find that journalism job. Or maybe it's politics that drives you wild? Then search for those opportunities in Washington, or consider working for a congressman in your district.

But for many of us, it takes a bit of soul searching to find the direction in which to point our job search. Katherine, an organization consultant, recalls:

> How did I discover my interests? I spent time reflecting, learning, discussing what matters to me, the legacy I want to leave, the contribution I'd like to make. I did this by participating in career, personal, and professional development classes, and by reading books of this nature.

Rebecca, a fundraiser who graduated from college in 2001, made a similar discovery.

> At the end of the day, it was over a drink with my best friend talking about the types of classes I'd taken and the extracurriculars I was involved with, and what made them interesting, valuable, and enjoyable, when I realized where I was headed.

You may not be the soul-searching type, but give it a shot. You'll change and so will your interests, but life will be so much better if you find a job that you find interesting and that doesn't bore you to tears.

But what if what you're interested in or passionate about doesn't come with any type of job security or a paycheck big enough to cover more than your grocery bills? That's a tough question, and we won't claim to know the right answer. But we

Ari's Corner

A passion for books and stories has always been a strong current running through my life. When I was twelve, a teacher introduced me to several outstanding African American authors. I then found a job at a bookstore specializing in ethnic literature. The owner became my friend and mentor, and for years we went to hear exceptional authors reading from their works. My work as a freelance writer after college was just the next step in following my passion for literature and storytelling.

have a few suggestions. Take some time and think about your priorities. Be brutally honest: Do you really want something bad enough to endure the many sacrifices in terms of lifestyle? Or is there a compromise you can find that would make more sense to you? For example, if your passion is to become a writer, you could find a more secure job, but one that leaves you enough time to work on the next great American novel. If you want to live in a relatively expensive city—say New York or San Francisco—have college loans, and would like to be able to eat something other than pasta every night, you'll have to be practical about balancing your interests and your job choices.

Nataly, a recent grad who started the company that published this book, offers this advice:

I had a ton of college loans after graduation, wanted to live in New York, and didn't have parents with deep pockets to support me. So I looked for jobs that were of interest to me but

Five Jobs in Five Years

by Nataly, Recent Grad and
Cofounder of NATAVI GUIDES
(the publisher of this very book)

I have an extremely coherent résumé. Really. After college I went to be a big-shot consultant at McKinsey & Co. After two years of slaving as a small-shot business analyst, I realized that I wanted a more hands-on job and one that allowed me to see sunlight from time to time, so I left to help run a start-up. Yes, a start-up, but one that miraculously survived the bubble and the bubble burst.

When the start-up was sold to a big, boring insurance company, I went looking for the next gig. Another start-up, but this time one that didn't last for more than a few months after I got there. Great timing on my part, but at least I had awesome coworkers.

I was out of college for three years, and I'd had three jobs. My résumé was starting to run over to the second page, and I was starting to think that hey, maybe sunlight wasn't that important after all.

But a few more career spin cycles were in my future. Through a chance meeting I ended up taking a job at a venture capital firm. A bit more sunlight than consulting, a bit more stability than start-ups. Not bad.

But I got the itch—to do my own thing. And I could only deny the urge for so long before I convinced my husband (read: partner in crime) to join me in starting a publishing company from our one-bedroom New York apartment. Wow, and I thought I knew what hard work was.

The moral of the story? You might not know what you want to do when you get out of college, but you will find it. Keep an open mind, don't discount any opportunities, and try to get as much as possible out of every job you have. My consulting days taught me how to think strategically; my start-up days, how to build a business from scratch; and my venture days, how to grow a business. No experience is a waste of time.

that came with some security, reasonable pay, and flexibility that would allow me to pursue my true passion for writing and publishing. We started our publishing company at nights and on weekends, using savings from our daytime jobs. I've also been able to work on a few books while being able to pay the bills and enjoy life in New York.

Don't buy into the "you're a sellout" rhetoric if you decide to take a job that pays and has some job security and pursue your true passions on the side. It's a naïve and idealistic way to look at the world. I've met people who refuse to "sell out" and who are miserable and tired of following their passions without any money or being able to support themselves.

The Spanish Self-Inquisition

No one ever said that choosing a job or a career path was easy. But you can make this process much more bearable if you get organized. (Yes, there is a method to this madness!)

You can go about getting organized in a hundred ways, but here's one suggestion—take from it what you find most helpful and adapt it to your particular situation. The general idea is this:

1. Think about your interests, skills, and priorities.
2. Consider your ideal work setting.
3. Identify several possible jobs.
4. Find several companies or organizations to go after.

Interests, Skills, and Priorities

Be self-obsessed for a bit. Before you think about what jobs you might like or what grand career path you'd like to follow, think about what you like, what you're interested in, what makes you go gaga excited, and what you'd like to spend your time doing. This means listening to what you already know from your lifetime of experiences (favorite hobbies, most compelling college classes, part-time jobs) and asking yourself a lot of questions, such as:

- What inspires me?
- What do I love to do?
- What are the skills I want to develop?
- What do I want to learn?
- What are my talents?

Once you've got the basics down, it's time for more specific questions regarding the components of various professions. Here are a few examples:

- Do I want to do a lot of writing? What kind of writing?
- Financial analysis? Or data entry?
- Do I want to teach? Or constantly learn?

- Evaluate other people's work?
- Speak in public?
- Do I want to spend my day on the phone?

After you have the beat on the type of work you'd like to do, take some time and think about your priorities. Do you want a job that makes you a ton of money so you can retire by the age of forty? Would you be more comfortable at a job that's pretty secure, or would you like to try some different things and take some risks? You get the idea—before you start looking for a job, have an idea of what you'd like out of your job and your life after college.

Work Setting

Next comes your preferred work setting. Think about what kind of an atmosphere you need to be most productive and happy. Or, just as important, are there certain settings that typically don't work for you? Here are some things to consider:

- Do I work best alone or in groups?
- Do I prefer short-term or long-term projects?
- Would I prefer working in an office or out in the field?
- Does a fast-paced work setting appeal to me?
- How do I deal with deadlines?
- How casual a work culture do I want?
- What kind of a work schedule do I want—9-to-5 or flexible?
- Will I want to work with people my own age?
- How diverse a work environment am I seeking?

Jobs

So, let's say, as an example, that you really like writing, prefer a fast-paced work environment, and would like to have other people around as you work. What types of jobs should you consider? Well, publishing jumps out right away. You could think about becoming a reporter for a newspaper or working in a big or small publishing house as an editor. But you may also consider going into radio or television broadcasting, where you could do a ton of writing and never lack a hectic, crazy work atmosphere.

The process of matching your interests to the actual jobs and careers you'll pursue is sometimes clear cut and sometimes not. A lot of it depends on how well you know what different jobs are out there and what they involve. Our advice is to put some work into this step. The more you know about the diversity of opportunities out there, the greater the chance that you'll go after those that you'll actually enjoy.

There are many books in your college career center, bookstores, and libraries that talk about the hundreds of different industries and the types of jobs that people in those industries have. Check 'em out. Another good idea is to browse online at the many job search websites, like www.monster.com or www.hotjobs.com—you can search by industry and then read the thousands of job listings and descriptions to get an idea of what they involve.

We'll talk about this more in the next chapter, but one of the best ways to learn about different jobs and what people in these jobs actually do all day is by talking to as many people as possible. Your college alumni, your parents and their friends, parents of your friends, and anyone else you can get in touch with can shed more light on what a certain job involves than countless books and online listings.

When doing research on potential jobs, try not to limit yourself. Explore, explore, explore. You want to know what's out there before you start narrowing down your options.

Company

Once you've narrowed down your list of potential jobs to a manageable size, you've got to start looking at companies and organizations where you might find those jobs. Your college or university might have a database of employers, or you can always use the extensive online job-listing websites, like www.monster.com.

Once you've found a few companies that interest you, become a snoop and find out as much as you can about them. Visit their websites, read news and reports about them, and if you can find an alum from your school or a friend of a friend of a friend who works there, see if you can talk to them for a few minutes. Even before you apply, you should try to know as much about a company as you can so that you don't end up wasting time applying to places where you'll be miserable.

Here are some questions to consider when researching specific companies:

- How big is the company?
- What's the working culture like?
- Is there a structured training program for entry-level employees?

- How is the company structured? Is it easy to go from one division to another?
- What types of people seem to work at the company (attitudes, education level, etc.)?
- What's the general atmosphere like?
- What does the company seem to stress as important employee qualities?
- How is it viewed in its industry?

These questions are by no means exhaustive, but they should give you a quick idea of some things to find out before you decide that a particular company might be a good place to apply for a job.

As you go through the exciting and frustrating process of figuring out where you want to work, keep notes. You might be one of those very annoying people who never forget anything, but you should write stuff down anyway. The sheer amount of information that's involved in a job search is overwhelming, and your notes will help you keep your sanity, at least to a degree.

Monica Lewinsky Was Right

In today's ultra-crazy, competitive job market, it helps to get a head start. While you're still in college, or if you can afford to after graduating, it pays to find internships. And not just for the connections you make, but for what these experiences reveal about real work, and about which job or industry may be right for you.

Sherie, a teacher, benefited in numerous ways from her intern experiences:

> One of the best pieces of advice that I got in college was to look for internship programs. These short internships gave me a taste of "life on the job" and helped me decide on my own career path. Also, in every interview I've had since, I've always been asked about my internship positions and what I did or learned.
>
> My internships helped me create a more well-rounded picture of my interests and abilities, as one was working at a TV news desk, another in a pharmacy, and yet others in teaching. They gave me a sense of what was expected in a professional job and the opportunity to interact with other professionals.

Will Work for Nothin'

In addition to internships, you can gain valuable experience and get a taste of the different jobs and industries by volunteering. This may mean shadowing someone whose work interests you, or spending a few hours of your own time learning the ropes in a variety of job settings.

Jason, a real estate agent in his twenties, firmly believes that:

> Gaining experience is the key. I would recommend trying to spend time with different people at different occupations. Actually shadow them on a daily basis to get an idea of the flow of the job. Waking up at the time they do, going home at the end of the day at the time they do, and realizing the commitment involved are essential to understanding what their job involves.

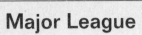

Major League

Remember your sophomore year of college, when everyone's favorite question was, "What's your major?" Back then it seemed like the most important decision in the world. Turns out, it can't compare to what flavor of Ramen to eat for dinner tonight. Seriously, don't let your major limit your job potential.

About 6 percent of the time, life is simple. If you had a pre-professional major, such as accounting, engineering, or premed, and if by the end of college it's still a field that you like, then good for you. You've cashed in on your 6 percent.

Most of us end up in the following category: You liked your major okay, but you can't figure out how it's supposed to score you a job that pays real money. We asked Brandi, a twenty-five-year-old who landed a job at a top-five management consulting firm after majoring in history, to share her insights.

Find the Firms that Want You

"I was looking for a career that would be lucrative but didn't require a specific scholastic background. I did a lot of research on different industries and found that management consulting was a career path that would suit someone like me. Through networking and informational interviews, I learned that most of the top firms were simply looking for well-rounded individuals who were smart and hard working. Bingo."

Play Up Your Relevant Skills

"The companies where I applied were most interested in my previous leadership experience and in my ability to work with others, rather than my specific major. So I geared my résumé to detailing some of my extracurriculars, as opposed to highlighting my coursework. Also, these companies needed experienced researchers with strong analytical skills, and my history major required these very qualities."

Learn How to Be a Good Learner

"Some firms have special recruiting programs for undergraduate and graduate students with nontechnical or professional degrees. They also sometimes offer extensive on-the-job training. So you don't necessarily have to know much about the field going in, but you must be able to catch on quickly."

Like many recent graduates, Brandi quickly realized that it's more often the actual skills you've developed in college that translate into jobs than the broad subject area that you studied. Hence, the difference between possessing exceptional writing skills and having been an English major—it's the writing ability and not your knowledge of Western literature that can lead you into areas such as marketing, editing, content management, teaching, or public relations.

If you loved your major and you still love it, follow that path. But if not, don't worry. Most people end up working outside the realm of their college focus.

Check with your college career center—they might have a shadowing program where you can arrange to spend time with some alumni as they go through their work day. We'll talk about informational interviews in the next chapter, but as you talk to experienced professionals in different fields, see if you can get enough guts to ask them if you could come and be their unobtrusive and discreet shadow for a day.

Ari's Corner

While in Mexico, I volunteered to help the host of a bilingual radio show, giving very brief news reports during his hour broadcast. One morning, I showed up fifteen minutes before we went on air and learned that the host had disappeared. One of the guests turned to me and said, "Give it a shot, kid. The show must go on." The fact that the highly improvised show wasn't a disaster led to a permanent position as host.

Be Promiscuous, Sort of

Sometimes we tend to think of a career path as a straight line, a logical sequence of jobs that all fall within a certain industry or area, and that we pursue one after another. But that's just one way to think about it, and frankly, from our own experiences and those of the hundreds of people we interviewed for this book, it's both a limiting and unrealistic way to think of your working future. If you're like most of us, your career path may have some, well, "exciting" and "unexpected" twists and turns.

Jason, the real estate agent from a few pages ago, adds another thought about shaping your career:

Depending on your educational background, it may be necessary to experience several jobs before a true career can form. Trying different jobs can be a huge benefit in helping you really figure out what you like and don't like to do.

Even those who are set on one particular career don't always end up living their vision. Not every would-be Tom Cruise, Bill Gates, Ernest Hemingway, or Barbara Walters finds fame and recognition. Meanwhile, others discover that their dream jobs aren't all they're cracked up to be.

Matt is a twenty-something writer and waiter in Brooklyn, NY. He provides this illustrative analogy:

> Visualize life as a funnel, with the skinny end pointing down and the open end up. Most of our lives until graduation have been lived in that small, narrow, straight tube, guided by choices that were made for us, such as where we lived, went to high school, and the fact that we went to college. But at that moment of college graduation, the world opens up into a giant funnel with its rim far off in the distance.
>
> My advice is this: Set your goals, whatever they may be, up on that rim, and never lose sight of them. Then take the wildest, craziest, most zig-zaggy-up-and-down path through as much of the interior of that funnel as you can possibly cover.

Marc is an author who seems to have taken this advice to heart—he has a job history that's all over the place.

> I dropped out of Yale and hit the road with my thumb stuck out, one change of clothes, and no "bread," trusting in synchronicity and guidance and whatever my soul called out for at the moment.
>
> I've done everything from working as a dishwasher at the Red Lion Inn to a New York City postal deliveryman to a Fuller

We Talk With . . .

Jay, Former College Counselor

What should people in college be doing now to better prepare themselves for the workforce?

If you want to get a job when you're done with college, one of the key critical things is to get good summer jobs during college. You can take a month and travel, but for the other month and a half you should get a job. If you don't know exactly what you're going to do after graduation, go and work in the field you have some interest in.

You should really look at what is fun for you. Because what is fun for you is what you enjoy. And what you really enjoy, if you can make that your career, you're going to be a happy person.

"Well, it's fun to drink beer." How fun? If beer really fascinates the living daylights out of you, check out the beer industry. That's fine. There are a lot of people who think work is unpleasant and play is fun, and that's unfortunate.

Are there any pitfalls to avoid?

Be very attentive when you say: I should do something. If you're saying, "I should, I should," it may not be what you're interested in. Think about "I want." This is the time to follow your interests.

What other advice would you like to share?

If you really don't know what you want to do, do something anyway. It doesn't matter if you're not sure, that's okay. Do something. Because everything you do, you learn and make friends. Making friends is making connections.

Brush Man to a day laborer mucking concrete to head chef at a Buddhist ski lodge in Wyoming.

You might be a free spirit like Marc, or you might follow a more traditional and organized career path after college. It's entirely up to you. Just remember to expect the unexpected and not be afraid to take a few detours or change your direction a few times. Don't feel like a failure if at one point you realize that what you'd always dreamed of doing brings you no satisfaction at all. This is your time to figure this stuff out—not when you're a fifty-year-old big shot so-and-so, miserable about your job and not having taken enough chances when you were younger.

Nabulungi, who took a position as an executive assistant after foregoing medical school, reminds us: "Be as open-minded as possible. Don't be bogged down by preconceived notions your parents may have about what is best for you."

No matter how many informational interviews you arrange or internships you secure, it takes time to gain a real sense of what you want. So stay receptive to a wide variety of job opportunities. What you learn as a waiter may help you as a marketing executive, and what you observe as a cashier can help you as a chief financial officer.

You're Not Alone

This whole job search process can get pretty stressful and overwhelming. But remember that you're definitely not alone, and you shouldn't feel like you have to make these big life decisions all on your own.

Some Jobs . . .
by Nils, Writer

The best way to find a job is to jump in and try something that you think you're interested in. Also understand that some jobs won't be fully nourishing to your mind, body, and soul. What I mean is that all work has different benefits and drawbacks—it's a compromise.

Some jobs are just about earning money so you can afford to do what you really like to do. Some jobs are boring, but the coworkers are great, so it's worth it. Some jobs are wonderful and you pour your heart into your work, but the pay is crap. Some jobs are terrible, but the schedule allows you to do other things (spend time with your partner, work on your art, whatever). Some jobs are no fun but are necessary stepping stones to good positions further down the road. Some jobs pay well, but the hours are so long that you can't spend time with the people you love. Every job is some sort of compromise.

I'd also make the following recommendations:

- Have fun in college.

- Take a class in accounting, keep track of your budget, and learn Microsoft Excel.

- Find role models who are in the out-of-college outside world. Talk to them and learn about what they're doing. Are they happy? Are they doing something you'd like to do?

- Try different jobs in the summer or during the school year.

Talk to people! Spend some time with a career counselor or two, get in touch with as many alumni and professionals as possible, and hey, talk to your friends who might be able to share some wisdom and an understanding ear.

Keep in mind that everyone has their own agenda, and don't feel like you have to accept every piece of advice that you hear. In fact, don't do that. But you can listen, get what you need, and then chart your own course.

Your job is your choice, but you don't have to make it alone.

Total Recall

- Professional growth and career answers take time, so don't panic if you have no idea what to do after college. Keep your options and mind open, and actively reflect on what you like or dislike about jobs as you move forward.

- Don't be afraid to take risks. Your career is an evolving process. It's never decided by your first job. Or your fifth, for that matter.

- When choosing a job and career path, first identify your interests and skills and your preferred work environment, and then look for jobs and companies that match your preferences.

- Choosing a job and a career path is like choosing a college. There are numerous questions involving lifestyle, location, pay, culture, and compatibility with who you are. Don't rush the decision.

- Internships and volunteering are excellent ways to gain experience, make contacts, and answer career questions during your college years and beyond.

- No matter how much research you do, you might have to hop around a bit before you find a job that you really like. And that's okay!

- Don't make huge life decisions in isolation. Talk to as many people as you can during your job search and gain the benefit of their experiences and advice. You don't have to take it all, but you might learn a thing or two to help you land a better job.

2

Yada Yada Yada

(or networking)

We're inherently social beings. And most of us are somewhat self-centered social beings. Which means we like to talk, and we especially like to talk about ourselves. (Cue flashbacks of your relatives at any holiday party, ever.)

Networking is easy and fun (stop shaking your head) because it taps into this human predilection to talk about ourselves when asked. Consider successful networking as little more than the process of guiding people to tell you about their life, what they're doing, the company that employs them, and their industry.

Who knew that so much could come from a simple conversation? Or even an email. But it can. And it does. Networking is literally the most effective way to find out about what different jobs are out there and what they involve, to research specific companies and industries, to meet a mentor, or join a peer group, and hey, even get a job.

Remember, networking is no more than meeting people, communicating with them, and then staying in touch (even as infrequently as once every year or two). It's that simple. Really. So let's get started.

- Ego-Tripping
- Old Boys Network, Minus the Old Boys
- Ask and You Shall Receive
- (Less Than) Great Expectations
- Lifetime Membership
- Conferences, Job Fairs, and Other Mortifying Experiences
- Mentors, the Fresh Makers
- Internetworking

Ego-Tripping

Networking can seem daunting and even scary. You might ask, Why would accomplished professionals want to speak to me? How could they even have the time or interest to do so? and What could they gain from our conversation?

First, stop beating yourself up. Second, listen to this insight from Eben, a twenty-six-year-old public relations associate in Washington, D.C.

People like to feel wanted and connected. So don't be shy. If you know someone who knows someone who can help get you a job, get on the phone and make the connection. It's a great ego-stroke for them and a good connection for you.

Ah, the ego. As Eben has highlighted, never underestimate the power of flattery. Networking puts people in a position of assisting through reflection. If you ask someone for help, more people will want to help than not. Guaranteed. As much as Hollywood would hate to admit it, most of the working world is nothing like the movies *Boiler Room* or *Wall Street*. So just ask.

Old Boys Network, Minus the Old Boys

It's okay if you find the whole venture of networking intimidating or overwhelming. Initially, it can be. Thinking about how to start a conversation, what to ask about someone's job, or how to follow up on an encounter can feel new and awkward. That's fine. But as with just about everything in life, you'll get better—rapidly.

Ben, an aspiring architect in Ohio, offers this overview:

Networking usually applies to conversing with older people in a profession you're interested in. I think it's a loaded word that carries horrible images of rich, white guys at country clubs with cigars, mustaches, and white tennis sweaters.

I remember being terrified when older students kept saying I should go to this or that event because there was a good opportunity for networking. After a while, I realized what networking is really all about: Old people like to be around young people.

Ben's Corner

When I first graduated from college, I networked with people connected to my parents, my high school, and my university. Which means I was never at a loss for conversation topics. Think about it. How easy is it to laugh about your parents' hippie days, that notorious eighty-year-old Latin teacher, or ridiculous exam-period traditions on campus?

The real world is full of serious situations, and most people in it long for the fun of their college days. Help them remember it. Introduce yourself. And be yourself—don't try to act like you're older or that you know something these people don't.

They know you don't know anything yet—you're too damn young. Instead, show them that you're full of energy and interested in what they do. Ask questions. Most people love to talk about what they spend forty hours a week doing.

Ask and You Shall Receive

Madeline, a veteran consultant for nonprofits, understands the extensive benefits to networking:

Almost every job I've had I've gotten from networking, word of mouth, or knowing someone. The key to success is connecting with people and joining a group of like-minded thinkers. Don't underestimate the power of maintaining relationships. Life is all about relationships.

Jamison, a faculty assistant at Harvard's Kennedy School, networked her way into exceptional internships and summer jobs during college, and then into full-time work after graduating in 2001. Here comes her advice, so uncap your highlighter now.

No Man Is an Island

"The hardest part of the networking process is beginning it. But once you start, the whole process seems to snowball on itself. Ask professors, friends, parents, family friends, and former employers for suggestions of people to talk to—not for a job but for information on finding a job in a given field. One person suggests two people to call, those two people suggest one more each, and pretty soon you have a wide range of contacts to assist you in the job-finding process."

Beware of the J-Word

"Something that's really important in the whole networking process is the wording that you use when approaching people. If you contact someone and present yourself as if you're asking for a job, you're likely to end the conversation before it begins. However, if you make it clear that you're really only looking for advice or guidance, people will be much more willing to help you."

Ben's Corner

Volunteering has been one of the most effective ways to expand my network. And best of all, it doesn't have the smarmy feel of asking for someone's business card while sipping Sapphire & tonics in a hotel bar. To expand my peer group, I simply found the organizations that attract the kind of people I wanted to meet. Where a person is employed or volunteers is one of the easiest ways to identify his or her values, goals, and connections.

The Informational Interview

"The term 'informational interview,' as cheesy as it is, was one that I threw around a lot when looking for a job. People don't want to be harassed about a job, but they're happy to talk to you and mentor you. These informational interviews are so important not just for finding a job but also for figuring out how to establish a career. If you look at your career path long term and consider all the steps required to get there, it's extremely useful to speak with someone who has already made the trip."

(Less Than) Great Expectations

One point to appreciate is that networking is no magic bullet. It takes more than one contact, typically, to have your résume read or to snag an interview. Unless your contact is the

Networking Topics

What you need to know about networking is that everybody does it. And what you'll find when you begin meeting with family friends or high school alums is that networking is a little bit like a first date.

Before someone is willing to open doors for you with a phone call or email, he wants to size you up and ensure you're okay. Why? Because he needs to be confident that you will represent him well. Why would someone want to do a favor for an idiot? Good news: You're not an idiot. But to help you feel more comfortable for your initial networking meetings, here are suggestions for some topics and questions you could cover.

Family Friend

Tell her about your interests, your goals, and what you've accomplished up to this point. Is there any advice that she can share? Does she have any suggestions regarding your job search? How did she decide on a career path after graduating from college?

Alumnus

Ask if there are ways that your school can facilitate networking and the job search. Are there alumni associations, meetings, or events that you can tap into? Listservs? People he knows offhand whom you could call or email? Are there specific companies or organizations with which your school maintains close ties? What opportunities has he pursued in his career?

Peer

Determine your common interests and see if she has concrete tips for you regarding the job search. What does she think about the personal development and growth opportunities at her current company? Are there classes you can take to make yourself a more competitive candidate for future openings? What was her first job like? Was the work challenging? How did her colleagues treat her?

Godfather. In fact, sans Sicilian blood, it usually takes five or more contacts. Which means you need to network with realistic expectations, persistence, and respect for the people who help you.

Sometimes, contacts will offer suggestions or connections that simply don't match your needs or goals. You mentioned an interest in marketing, and your aunt suggests you speak with her friend who teaches first grade. It happens.

But a cardinal rule of networking is to respect your contact and to honor the relationship. This means you need to call your aunt's friend the teacher. Who knows? Perhaps she'll have connections to marketing firms that your aunt never knew about. Regardless, appreciate the fact that these people are doing you a favor. Humor and trust them, and follow up on their suggestions, no matter how seemingly irrelevant. Who knows what could come of it?

Lifetime Membership

Don't misunderstand the purpose of networking—it's not solely for the job search. Envision it as more of a special peer

We Talk With . . .
Lee, Screenwriter

Why network?

Particularly in Hollywood, you can never know enough people. Also, when you're first starting off in any industry, you want to meet many people for all sorts of reasons: to learn more about the comings and goings of the industry, new trends, and maybe even job openings that you didn't know existed.

Also, people don't like to make decisions on their own. There's nothing better for a human resources director than to hear that someone else in the company vouches for a particular candidate. Networking is a skill, and it's as important to career growth as strong writing skills or an analytical mind.

How have you networked?

I've combed alumni listings, spoken to every long-lost relative in other people's families, and emailed patrons from a restaurant I worked at for a summer. Personally, I'm not a fan of networking parties; I'm much better at one-on-one.

What are the keys to successful networking?

Be fearless. You have to realize that people love to help. It makes them feel powerful and better about themselves. Be persistent. Follow up. Call anyone who might be helpful, even if you don't have high expectations for it to "pan out." They might know someone who knows someone. Offer to take *them* out. Grab a drink, keep it casual, and let the conversation steer toward your intended goal. Be aware of when to cash in your favors. People are willing to help, but make it count.

Are there things you shouldn't say when networking?

You shouldn't ask for a job. Keep it informational. If people are interested or know of a job, they'll mention it.

group, people with whom you maintain relationships when you're working (or not) for reasons of professional growth, connections, and just having someone to ask for advice as you navigate through your career maze.

Barbara, a regional president for Magellan Health Services, explains that:

> Networking is an important part of developing and maintaining a robust professional life. As you think about potential jobs and when you are in a job, realize that you're always networking—building relationships, making connections, and exploring what possibilities might be available.
>
> Remember, people like being asked for their opinions and many times willingly provide assistance. View networking as windows of opportunities to gain information and build connections. You never know when those connections will come into play.

Mike, a neophyte fund accountant with Mellon Financial, seconds this advice, and encourages networking with colleagues:

> One good way to network once you're in a company is to participate in social functions with coworkers and managers outside of work. A charity golf outing, fundraising events, or volunteer work are good examples—and don't forget holiday parties. People are sometimes less stressed around the holidays and more likely to be in good spirits.

Lastly, Jerome, a consultant and former CEO, underscores the importance of diversifying and expanding your peer group in the new economy. He says:

Networking early in your career, it's better to not limit yourself to just people in the industry you work in, since these days people are more likely to have several jobs in the same or different industries over time.

Some of your best networking opportunities arise when you're employed, as implied by Barbara, Mike, and Jerome. Use your connections through work to make others. A strong and expansive network of peers, friends, colleagues, and mentors is a huge component of your career success.

Conferences, Job Fairs, and Other Mortifying Experiences

First, that title is a joke. Conferences and job fairs are not mortifying, because there isn't anything easier than meeting people at a conference or a job fair since both kinds of events are literally made for networking. Pause for a moment to consider how easy striking up a conversation could be at a conference of any kind:

- What did you think of that last panel discussion?
- What attracted you to this conference?
- Which afternoon session will you be attending?
- How are you enjoying these revolting turkey sandwiches?

Job fairs can spook some people because we imagine a day of grueling, competitive interviews and selling yourself on the spot in thirty seconds. The suits, the résumés in hand, a make-or-break interview, a parched throat, the sweaty palms . . . c'mon now, this is no time to develop an ulcer.

Instead, envision job fairs as an excellent way to gather information, to chat with human resources representatives from various companies, and to potentially arrange follow-up opportunities (even an interview, if it so happens).

Due to people whom you meet or details you learn at an event, your cover letters and interviews will convey a greater level of preparedness, interest, and research. These events will give you an edge over other applicants.

Just remember three key tips for making the most of job fairs and conferences: First, go alone (otherwise, you won't meet anybody). Second, keep your own business cards in an easily accessible and lint-free location on your body. Third, go alone.

Mentors, the Fresh Makers

One of the most important things you should aim to do while networking is to find a mentor who will help you shape your career. Mentors are essentially professional coaches, people invested in facilitating your development as an individual.

For reasons of experience and wisdom, a mentor tends to be older. And simply put, it's critical to your long-term success to find a supportive and dedicated mentor. Hang on. Allow us to repeat this point: It's critical to your long-term success to find a supportive and dedicated mentor.

Eva, a twenty-seven-year-old development associate, shares some advice:

Avenues for Networking
by Kelly, Research Associate

I network through prior business contacts, alumni contacts, local networking groups, and bars.

Prior Business Contacts
Ask anyone you know in the industry if they have any contacts in the area. Ask friends if they know anyone in your location or industry. They can introduce you by email or call a friend. Then you can follow up by email or phone to set up an introductory phone conversation or face-to-face meeting.

Alumni Contacts
Don't underestimate the power of alumni contacts. You can look on an alumni database, contact a career services office, or research local alumni clubs in your current location. Attend functions and meetings and try to get involved. Even if alumni are not in your field, they may be well connected and can then refer you to others in your industry.

Local Networking Groups
Look online and in local magazines and newspapers for networking groups. There are clubs everywhere for different interests. There are also organized social clubs for hobbies and sports (rugby, softball, ultimate Frisbee, etc.), which newcomers are welcome to join. Many people find jobs through casual encounters in an informal setting where business dialogue is more natural.

Bars
Go out to bars—and feel good about it. Find out the popular spots and socialize with people over drinks. Ask people casually

for advice. What have they done in a job hunt? What worked for them? I've gotten three interviews from random encounters. Again, this type of dialogue is much more natural in a bar setting.

Find an informal mentor who's available to talk about the process of finding a job or deciding to go back to school. This person can also help by commenting on your résumes and cover letters. A second opinion from someone who has a commitment to your future will double your confidence when contacting potential employers.

Marc is an associate director for fundraising who completed graduate school in 2001. He takes Eva's advice to another level, asserting that often one mentor is not enough:

Find a mentor—identify someone with whom you can talk candidly about life issues. One person probably won't be able to accommodate all of these things, so it may be prudent to have, for example, a different mentor for professional matters, your social life, spiritual issues, and financial guidance.

Mentors can also help you network better by introducing you to their social and professional circles, which is ideal. Most often, our peers and friends at other companies will not be in a position to hire or to significantly sway hiring decisions. What do you expect—they're still young. But one of your mentor's peers, on the other hand, could be the Director of Human Resources. You get the point. Now get a mentor.

Internetworking

Who said networking could only happen outside the comforts of your own home? Remember, we're Generation.com and the Internet is our friend. Network online, in nothing more than underwear if you wish, in the following ways:

- Post your résumé on www.careerbuilder.com
- Participate in message boards on www.monster.com
- Scan for job fairs on www.employmentguide.com
- Peruse local networking event listings on www.craigslist. org

Okay, so we lied. Only the first two ideas allow you to network in your underwear the entire time. But at least we offered you some choices.

Another avenue is your college. An obvious route, yet consistently underutilized. Don't think dropping a hundred grand was for nothing. Alumni networking is low-hanging fruit. Visit your school's website, check out the alumni section, and find out what's happening in your region and when.

Total Recall

- Don't feel awkward about networking. It's a normal process that is expected and common.

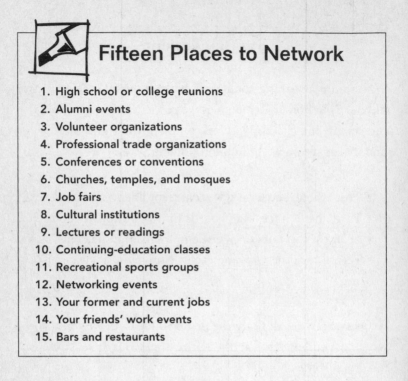

Fifteen Places to Network

1. High school or college reunions
2. Alumni events
3. Volunteer organizations
4. Professional trade organizations
5. Conferences or conventions
6. Churches, temples, and mosques
7. Job fairs
8. Cultural institutions
9. Lectures or readings
10. Continuing-education classes
11. Recreational sports groups
12. Networking events
13. Your former and current jobs
14. Your friends' work events
15. Bars and restaurants

- Network with people from your everyday life: friends, family, peers, and alumni.

- When networking, ask lots of questions, volunteer personal information, and arrange informational interviews.

- Never directly ask for a job when you're networking. Ask for advice and information, and a job opportunity might present itself later on.

- Don't discount any contact or opportunity—you never know where it might lead you.

- Maintain positive relationships with your contacts by respecting them, respecting their contacts, and by following up with them in the manner you agree upon.

- Maintain and grow your professional network as you progress in your career. It's an invaluable asset.

- Finding a mentor won't happen overnight, but it's something you should aim for. Mentors can share great advice, open up doors, and help you score your next gig.

- Internetwork: Get online, post your résumé, view job fair announcements, peruse advertisements for local networking events, hit message boards, and find out when your next college alumni event is happening nearby.

3

Playing the Game

(or applying and interviewing)

Congratulations! Through your networking, industry research, and deals with the devil, you've managed to score yourself some concrete leads in this quest to reach the end of the job-search labyrinth. Now it's time to apply for positions. If that sounds scary, it is—at least a little. The mere notion of having to explain why you deserve a paycheck from an employer when you may not have enough of anything that they're looking for is, well, not a pleasant thought.

But the good news is that everyone who will be reading your résumé and posing the tough questions has also stood in your beat-up tennis shoes. They've had to apply for positions and may be more sensitive to your concerns than you think. Take a deep breath, put on your confident face (and a nice suit), and dive into it.

Nobody Said Snooping Was Illegal

If you thought that you were done with homework now that you've finished narrowing down your job search, boy, were you wrong. As Barbara, a health care executive in her fifties, suggests, "Do your homework and understand as much as possible about the job prior to sending in your application."

What might that homework consist of? Quite a bit, actually. If the company has a website (and which one doesn't?) check it out. And this means hitting the "About Us" section like nobody's business. Read through the objectives of the organization as a whole, and make sure that you understand exactly what it does and for whom.

- What are the company's mission, services, and products?
- Have strategies changed within the past six months, year, or decade? If so, how?
- Who are the competitors of this company, and how do they compare with this company? (Pssst, that's your clue to also view the websites of competing organizations. Thank us later.)

Is there a section on the company website exhibiting recent press or news stories about it? Find this section, because these articles are one of the best ways to ascertain an organization's recent and future developments, innovations, and achievements. If the website doesn't have much in the way of news, then it's time to hit the search engines.

You must Google the company, since web searches and on-line investigation will lead to a more substantive cover letter and a more informed interview. Imagine how you'd look if you were the only applicant who noticed a recent laudatory article in the *Washington Post*? Really frickin' good.

Make sure you've researched most, if not all, of the following areas of your target company before starting a cover letter:

- Company history and basic stats
- Mission, values, and vision
- Goals, objectives, and overall strategy
- Areas of expertise
- Board and committee members
- Corporate partnerships
- Community involvement
- Competitors and status within industry
- Recent news, developments, and projects

Reading Between the Lines

An important skill to develop is reading the subtext of job postings. Say wha'? By paying close attention to the language in a posting, we can learn a substantial amount about a company and what it's like to work there. Take a peek at this posting from www.monster.com:

In more than 135 countries around the globe, our people operate with the highest levels of integrity, quality, and professionalism, providing clients with solutions based on financial, transactional, and risk-management knowledge of audit, tax, and corporate finance.

We strive to help all of our people achieve both their professional and personal goals through an inclusive environment that values everyone's contributions, appreciates diversity of thought, fosters growth, and provides continuous opportunities for development.

The Paralegal hired into this position would work with client serving professionals, assisting with document management, research, and administrative aspects of litigation engagements.

Company Overview

First of all, does working for a global corporation appeal to you? If you were to apply for a position there, do you have past academic or professional experiences that demonstrate your familiarity with the expectations of a corporate workplace? If you don't have a corporate background, would you be bringing something else to the job that is unique, such as experience in the nonprofit sector or specialized knowledge from a smaller firm?

Company Culture

Most of us want a job that allows for and expects professional growth. This job description explicitly states that this value is part of the work atmosphere at this company. This second paragraph can answer numerous questions an applicant may have regarding professional development, hierarchy, and overall office culture. Remember the self-inquisition we suggested in the first chapter? If you have specific work-setting preferences, this part of the job listing can give you a clue about what to expect.

Job Requirements

Let's be real for a moment: Do you have the experience this company is requesting? If not, that's okay. But do you have previous work or academic experience that could be relevant to the strengths needed for this paralegal position (such as exceptional research and writing skills)?

When considering an open position such as this one, think generally about the skills you may have employed or learned throughout college, in summer jobs, or during an internship. Do these abilities relate to the "document management, research, and administrative" responsibilities required of a paralegal at this company?

Don't fret if you're not sure you're the cookie cutout a company is seeking. Perhaps you've never held a position similar to the one that is being offered, but that doesn't mean you don't have skills that will be assets to the job. To many people's surprise, most professional talents and skills are applicable in numerous industries.

Read This Disclaimer

Job listings are the company's way of selling a position. Be cautious about taking everything you read at face value. Use this information as a starting point, but don't rely on it entirely.

Know a lot about where you're applying and target your cover letter, résumé, and what you say during your interview based on that information. Your chances of success will go way up.

Cover the Basics

Now's the fun part—using what you've learned. There's no good reason to research a company's recent accomplishments, reflect on an organization's mission and values, or contrast a firm with others in the industry unless you can use this information in your application for a position. Your mom might be very impressed with your insights and knowledge, but she's not hiring.

Before you can get into that office and wow them with your winning smile, you have to sell yourself with good, old-fashioned pen and ink. Well, more like printer paper and inkjet.

Cover letters accompany your resume and do the job of introducing you and your qualifications to your potential employer. The key word here is *introduction*—you don't want to write too much. Think of it as a "foot-in-the-door" letter. It should be concise (about half a page of text) and compelling.

Ben, the architect who learned to network without a tennis sweater, gives a good recipe:

One, say who you are and why you're interested in their firm. Two, tell a little about yourself. Three, say you will call on a specific date (about a week after the letter arrives) to discuss how you can benefit the company. Four, thank them for their time.

A Good Cover Letter

Dear Ms. Yao,

Just this morning, I encountered your Development Associate job posting on Idealist.org.[1] As a Boston native with ties to community development groups, I am familiar with YouthGrow America and its history of urban impact through programs for young adults. I care deeply about the support of underserved populations and neighborhoods in the area, and I want to contribute to your mission.[2]

For the past year, I have worked at ConstructioNeeds, an Internet company for the construction industry. My position at this dot-com couldn't have prepared me better for a development role in your organization. At ConstructioNeeds, I was contacting and introducing new users to our service through sales and customer service calls, email campaigns, targeted faxes, and direct mailings. Due to the traditional ways of the construction industry, I had to rely on strong communication skills and creative marketing to solicit activity and equipment quotes on our site. But with persistence, some innovative tactics, and regular data analysis, I ultimately drew around $50 million in quotes from our users over the course of a year.[3] Yet while this experience bolstered my abilities, from sales and marketing, to writing and editing, to customer support and data management, it lacked a sense of real social value. Now I seek a position that is both intensive and socially meaningful.[4]

YouthGrow America catalyzes low-income communities by educating and training their youth. Not only do I want to join a group that stimulates this kind of development in under-resourced areas, but I also hope to direct similar efforts on my own in several years. The issue of inner-city community growth matters to me enormously, and this social concern will eventually lead me to business school. I hope to begin this journey with YouthGrow America.[5]

Thank you for your time, and I will call you in a week to follow up.

Sincerely,

John Smith

1. John immediately states how he heard of the position. Even the phrase "just this morning" carries a great deal of weight, as it shows how quickly he acted once he learned of the job opening.

2. By the end of paragraph one, he has explicitly stated that he is interested in the job and has given a bit of personal background to support why the position appeals to him.

3. Here, John is supporting his general statement of being qualified for the development job with impressive facts about his previous position. We see that he has experience relevant to fundraising, and even someone unfamiliar with the construction industry can marvel at a $50 million figure.

4. If John was such a fabulous employee at ConstructioNeeds, perhaps the reader of the cover letter may be wondering why he left the position. He gives an excellent explanation here, stating his desire for a job that carries more impact on the community. It again substantiates his claim in the opening paragraph that he is tremendously interested in improving the city.

5. John shares with the potential employer some of his plans for the future, plans that could benefit from a partnership with YouthGrow America. He even mentions grad school, which may seem like a bad idea being that he may have to leave the company, but his ambition and passion combine to make his conclusion honest and compelling.

Another Good Cover Letter

Dear Mr. Wallace:

As a Boston native, I have grown up with NPR; the organization and its programming have substantially impacted my life. For this reason, I am very enthusiastic in applying for the Paralegal position as posted on npr.org. I possess significant experience in the legal field, and I view this opportunity as a unique way to contribute to an organization that has enriched my life for over 20 years. I was excited to find a position so well-tailored to my strengths, interests, and values, and through the advice of Tom Vallence, Senior Publicist for NPR, I have chosen to apply.

As my enclosed résumé highlights, I have gained a variety of work experiences both domestically and internationally. Most recently, I worked as a paralegal at a law firm specializing in immigration law. I assisted four attorneys in drafting numerous legal documents and forms for submission to the Department of Homeland Security and the State Department. Over the course of two years, I also managed more than 100 cases independently, working closely with over 30 different clients and federal agencies. In addition, I regularly performed extensive research on legal issues, monitoring changes in immigration law post–September 11th, and I collected data for country-specific asylum cases, compiling the information into a report detailing current issues affecting each country.

I can bring reliability, a strong work ethic, and a positive attitude to your organization. Due to my experience in a wide array of workplaces, I work very well both in groups and independently, and I am particularly adaptable to the pressure of changing deadlines. I wish to work in an environment of mutual respect with people who take pride in their work and

> where I feel I am making a significant contribution. I believe
> WGBH can provide such an opportunity.
>   Thank you for your time and consideration. I will follow up
> with you in a week to further discuss my qualifications.
> Sincerely,
> John Smith

Simple, right? Not always, so keep reading for some more detailed suggestions.

To Whom? I Am Concerned

Always address the letter to a specific person. It has more power than a "To Whom It May Concern" note. If you don't have a name, call the company and get one. And don't shoot yourself in the leg with silly mistakes like spelling the person's name wrong. Spellings can be double-checked by calling the firm. So can gender. Unisex names must be confirmed.

Always begin with who you are; why, specifically, you're interesting in working at the company; and for what position you're applying. If you have a contact within the organization, it's a good idea to mention that person as early as possible.

Also, if you became familiar with a company through an information session, job fair, or something of that nature, you should state this immediately. If there is someone inside their walls who remembers you, your letter might move to the top of the pile.

State how your experience, skills, or interests will make you a good match for their working environment. Cover letters must persuade the reader by clearly linking your skills and experience to the position for which you're applying.

Damola, a human resources assistant in her twenties, speaks to this very issue:

One thing I really see lacking is people doing their homework when they're job searching. For instance, people often send general inquiry resumes, and we don't do very much with them. On the other hand, when they go to our website and find specific positions to apply to, their resume has a much higher chance of being seen by a hiring manager.

You get the point—make your cover letter as personal and customized to each particular company as possible. The less generic it sounds, the better your chances of grabbing someone's attention.

Playing Telephone

To conclude your letter, provide a future date when you'll be in touch with the company to discuss matters further, unless the company is not accepting phone calls from applicants (which is common). The follow-up, if calls are welcomed, is done by phone about one to two weeks after the letter has been received.

Once you get someone on the phone, ask him or her any

A Terrible Cover Letter

To Whom It May Concern,[1]

I was at a party my mom was having and I met a friend of hers who works for your company. She made her job sound really fun and interesting, and I thought I would write to see if there are any positions available for a bright, eager young person like me.[2]

I graduated from College USA this past May with a degree in anthropology, but I haven't been able to find anything in my field. I'm going to apply to graduate school for next year, but in the meantime I am looking for a position where I can grow and learn new things. And who knows? Maybe I'll decide that anthropology is not for me.[3]

Though I'm not too familiar with what goes on in the corporate offices of your company, I shop in your retail stores all the time. It would be exciting to work as a buyer for such a cool store. I wouldn't even mind working as a buyer's personal helper (getting coffee, making calls, etc.). I've done this in summer jobs before.[4]

I sincerely hope that you have a job for me in your offices that fits as well as the clothes in your stores do![5]
Thank you,
Jane Brown

1. Jane clearly skipped the Cover the Basics section in this chapter. You should always address the letter to the appropriate person at the company. A little extra research makes you look a lot more prepared.

2. This first paragraph reads like a note to one of Jane's friends—there is no professionalism in her tone. Also, she completely wastes an excellent way to get her foot in the door—a personal contact. If you know someone who works

for the company, use his or her name and be specific about the things you learned from that person. Lastly, you should have a sense whether the company is hiring in the first place. And if you don't know this, you should at least have a suggestion about where you might be useful.

3. Poor Jane. She has managed to convey her flakiness in just one brief paragraph. Already we're envisioning her changing her major eight times and half-heartedly conducting a job search. Your academic history should make you appear driven, and it should compliment the position for which you're applying. It's also a terrible idea to admit that you're looking for a job simply to fill some time before you find something you really like.

4. Though we've suspected it from the first sentence, it's confirmed that Jane has done absolutely no homework on this company. She is wearing her youth on her sleeve by painting herself as a ditzy shopaholic who believes that it's possible to gain a buyer position with absolutely no experience. More realistically, Jane would be hired to perform menial tasks for someone at the company, which she does allude to. She briefly gets on the right track when she mentions prior work experience as an administrative assistant. But there is no detail to validate her claim.

5. While a well-placed, humorous statement could endear you to the reader, it's a poor idea when the tone is already so casual. Also, Jane seems like she wants to skip right to the hiring process. It would've been in her best interest to ask for an informational interview, since she doesn't have much of a clue about . . . much of anything.

questions that could help bolster your application. As Ben, our cover-letter guru, explains,

> Many young people are terrified of calling strangers. There's no reason to get upset if someone you call is rude or disagreeable. If they are, then you can be certain it's a work environment you don't want to be a part of. Simply thank them for their time and hang up.
>
> I try to ease this process by calling firms when I am completely naked or in my underwear. This usually makes me less nervous.

Uh, thanks Ben. We can all see that you've found ways to boost your, um, sense of self. But seriously—don't be intimidated when making follow-up calls. It's not always pleasant, but that one call that goes great and leads to an interview will make up for most others.

Jeff, a fledgling music producer, calls companies *before* applying, not after. He uses somewhat stealthy phone calls to get the low-down on companies he's considering. After sufficient research on a firm, he suggests selecting one or two jobs that appear most appealing. Then,

> Call them and say that you're interested in interviewing someone from the company because you're interested in the industry. And let them know you're not presently seeking a job in the field. This statement will put them and you at ease. Most companies and executives are happy to fill these kinds of requests since they enjoy talking about their industry.

Rachel's Corner

During a summer in college, I worked at a design firm where the secretary had just quit. I took over all of her responsibilities for three months. The most useful skill that I gained in those three months? I learned to give good phone. Phone etiquette is required for almost every job you can think of. People on the other end are judging you on your tone, your word usage, and your ability to be clear and concise. The only downside of my receptionist position was that I started answering the phone at home with my standard work greeting: "Good afternoon, this is Rachel speaking, how may I help you?" But once I deprogrammed myself, I was left with a phone demeanor that can knock any professional's socks off.

And once you talk to someone—well, there's your personal contact!

Another sneaky way to get your foot in the door at a company is through temping, especially since many companies hire their capable temps into full-time positions. Not only does temping allow you an insider's view of the office culture and atmosphere, but it also brings you into the loop regarding current hiring needs. Temping is far from rocket science, but it could literally get you an entry-level job at your first-choice company. Here's what you do:

- Step one: Call that company's Human Resources department and ask which temp agency they use.
- Step two: Sign up with that very temp agency.

- Step three: Specify to the temp agency in which company you want to be placed.
- Step four: Snag a sweet job at your preferred company and thank us later.

Minority Report

Most employers have some system of affirmative action in place to ensure diversity in the workplace. So if you're a woman, an ethnic minority, or both, with qualifications for the position— because no one is hiring simply based on gender or race—you should use these characteristics to your advantage.

Publicity

No one can give you a leg up if they don't know that you're a minority. If you have a unisex name, find a way to clarify that you're a woman. You could use the prefix "Ms." in your cover letter, for instance. If you're a person of color, you can mention an organization to which you belong.

Keith, a doctor in his late twenties, remembers his days of applying to summer internships in college. "You can't just come out and write, 'I'm black, by the way.' I used to include in my résumé that I was an officer in my school's Black Student League. That made it clear."

Then again, other circumstances can elicit a more candid approach. Jerry, an entrepreneur in his mid-twenties, states it simply: "For years, I've been involved with a group that helps East Asian children. When I first contacted the group, of course I talked about being Chinese. Duh."

Context

Know when to play up your uniqueness, and know when it's not so special. For example, if you want to be an elementary school teacher, being a woman is not going to impress the hiring committee. But in a male-dominated industry such as finance, that's a different story.

When Kelly, a corporate twenty-six-year-old, was applying to business school, she wrote an entire essay about the women's networking group that she established at her financial services company. "It was the first thing admissions officers asked me about in my interviews."

Not a Woman, Not an Ethnic Minority

You can still be a minority in certain situations. Perhaps an employer is looking for geographical diversity, or maybe the company wants a staff person who has varied academic backgrounds. You, like everyone else, should be highlighting those traits that make you stand out from the pack.

The Résume: Just How Important Is It?

Pretty darn important. Why? It's a magical, one-page document that, if done correctly, can give a potential employer more information than, say, a PBS documentary on your life story. That may be an exaggeration, but the résume (also sometimes called a C.V.) should be a user-friendly way to figure out what you're about and if you're someone worth bringing in for an interview.

Before we even get into what the résumé should say, let's talk about what it should look like. Appearance does count, and there are ways to draw in a reader, or to turn him or her off, just by the layout of the page. According to Luam, an information technologist in New York, "My company has disregarded résumés of qualified applicants simply because the page looked disorganized."

- You don't want your résumé to be too congested or overly complicated.
- Stay away from a variety of fonts.
- Use indentations to mark subtopics.
- Whatever you do in terms of format, be consistent about it. The description of each job and extracurricular activity should be formatted exactly the same way—if you put your position in italics, you should put it in italics throughout the résumé.
- Use short, direct phrasing. For example, instead of writing "I taught English to a seventh-grade class in a large middle school located in the heart of the city," you can bullet, "Taught 7th grade English in large, urban middle school."
- Another tip that may prevent you from looking like an amateur: Place your previous work experience *before* your educational background. Many recent grads often do the opposite, but you shouldn't.

Okay, now on to what you should and should not include on your résumé. For example, should you list the paper route you had ten years ago? Um, no. As young people, we often feel like we don't have enough work or life experience to fill

We Talk With . . .

Aisha, Assistant Television Producer

What advice would you give to someone who is finishing school and about to begin the application process?
Make a promise to yourself at the beginning of senior year that you'll begin sending out five or six or ten cover letters and résumés a week, and do it. Do it as religiously as you do your homework.

If you can, go online, look at the company roster, and pick a specific person to whom to send your letter. If that information is not available, send it to Human Resources and keep your fingers crossed. Use all avenues—send your résumé to your aunts and uncles, listservs you belong to, whatever.

This is not the time to be shy.

If you're lucky enough to score an interview, any tips?
Research the company. Be prepared to answer, "Why do you want to work here as opposed to other companies?"

Have a friend interview you to practice. Recite your answers in the shower.

Make eye contact, smile, and afterwards, keep your fingers crossed and send a thank-you card.

up a good résumé. So we start grabbing at straws, putting in every single job we've ever had, even if it was cutting grass for your grandma.

While it's great to be able to boast a varied job background, you should cater your content to what the position you want requires. Choose jobs, volunteer work, community activities, and travel experiences that provided you with skills that could be used in future employment situations.

But while the paper route might be too far in the past to matter, sometimes those not-so-sophisticated positions may be more valuable than you thought. "Being a manager at McDonald's requires leadership, time management, and social skills. Don't feel like your jobs are too menial to include," says Rhonda, a young hospital liaison in Baltimore.

References, Hobbies, and Other B.S.

Employers usually ask for references if they're interested in contacting them. Don't waste space by including them on your résumé unless they were specifically requested. When you choose references, diversify the list by including past employers, professors, and people whom you know and who know you more personally.

When selecting your personal references, don't pick your favorite gossip partner unless the two of you also engage in more worthwhile activities, such as community service groups or sports teams. And always let people know if you listed them as a reference, both as a courtesy and a heads-up.

Sometimes people choose to include their hobbies at the bottom of their résumé. This may or may not be a good idea. Only include them if they're particularly unique and reveal clear facets of your personality that could be seen as assets to the company. Not everyone has been skydiving, for instance, and it suggests a daring, confident personality, which could be appealing to an employer. Often your interviewer will break the ice by talking about your hobbies, so make sure that they really are things you're interested in and you can discuss them with enthusiasm.

If you're the average movie-going, video game–playing, Internet surfer, you can presume that listing those activities won't make your résumé any more dazzling—unless, of course, you're applying to intern in your parents' living room.

Résumé Makeovers

It's kind of a cruel joke: In order to give you the perfect job, employers need to look at your résumé of less-than-perfect jobs. The trick? Lie about your jobs, of course. Or not.

All you really need is a résumé makeover. Take your subpar work experiences and make them sound like you're ready to ascend to CEO. The key is your use of detail, making the position appear selective, and highlighting personal responsibility. But don't go overboard: Overdressing your duties in a job is as obvious as wearing a toupee. Here are a few suggestions:

Before

Camp Counselor
- Taught swimming and crafts to kids at an overnight camp.
- Taught art class to campers twice a week.

Rockin' References

Prep Yourself

When you interview with a potential employer, you should always bring a nicely formatted sheet of paper with three references for the employer to call. For each listed reference, include a full name, title, company, phone number, email address, and relationship to you.

Prep Your References

But before you even get to that interview and before you even hand your interviewer a reference list, call or email the individuals you're listing as job references. You'd be amazed what a difference it makes when a job reference is expecting a phone call on your behalf.

When you contact your references, begin by explaining the company and the position for which you're applying. Next, detail what the potential employer is looking for. The more specific you can be, the better, because it could help that person tailor his or her answers and comments to the position you've described. If you feel comfortable, suggest to your reference which of your traits and experiences it might be useful to highlight—usually people won't mind a gentle nudge like that, as long as you don't go overboard.

The reality check is that your references can say whatever they want. Potential employers might ask about your weaknesses or areas in need of improvement on the job.

Prep Your Interviewer

Don't miss your opportunity at the end of an interview to explain your reference list to your interviewer. Clarify what kind of feedback each reference can provide and what types of projects or work to ask each person about. (This makes you look really good.)

After

Youth Instructor
- Taught basic, intermediate, and advanced swimming techniques and water safety to a class of 40 eight-year-old campers for 10 hours each week.
- Designed curriculum and lesson plans for daily arts and crafts course at the camp, and implemented them with a class of 30 ten-year-old campers. The course became a permanent fixture at the camp.

Before

Intern
- Learned about financial sector in an internship at a major financial corporation.
- Supported staff.

After

Financial Training Program Intern
- Was selected from a pool of 500 applicants for one of ten internships for undergraduates at a *Fortune* 100 investment firm in Philadelphia.
- Collaborated with senior staff members while learning the basics of financial accounting, modeling, and projections.

Before

Assistant
- Ran errands for a producer on the set of a major movie.

Résumé: Education

First, remember to put your education after your work experience. While a seemingly minor point, this formatting choice is but one more way to deemphasize your youth.

Second, don't overdo the details regarding your education. In the case of describing your educational background, less is more. Remember that a hiring manager is going to read your entire resume in about 30 seconds. So make it readable, clear, and strong.

Good

Dartmouth College, Hanover, NH
Bachelor of Arts, May 2003
Major: Economics, GPA: 3.75 out of 4.0
Senior thesis: *John Maynard Keynes and the Rise of Krispy Kreme: How Doughnuts Have Revolutionized U.S. Employment, Interest, and Money*

Not So Good

Dartmouth College
Hanover, NH
1999-2003
Graduated on May 25, 2003, in the class of 2003
Majored in Economics, while taking a diversity of other classes, such as Multivariate Calculus, Cellular Biology, European History, and Introductory Czech
Senior Thesis: *John Maynard Keynes and the Rise of Krispy Kreme: How Doughnuts Have Revolutionized U.S. Employment, Interest, and Money*
Grade Point Average: 3.75

Activities: Student Council, Students for a Free Tibet, Writing Tutor, Intramural Volleyball, Jazz Band, and Phi Tau Fraternity Rush Chairperson

Look at how confusing and crowded this education section is. *Don't do this.* **As stated before, less is more.**

After

Production Associate

- Supported staff and crew on set of $100 million summer blockbuster for the third-largest Hollywood production company.
- Shadowed executive producer of the film and was entrusted with duties critical to the smooth and successful operation of day-to-day activities.

Before

Candy Striper

- Cheered up sick children in the hospital by keeping them company and playing games.

After

Children's Hospital Volunteer

- Spent 15 hours per week in the pediatric oncology wing, lifting the spirits of young people diagnosed with cancer.
- Assisted hospital staff with patient care and support.

Résume: Employment Experience

Here are some additional examples of ways to describe entry-level positions or job-ish experiences common to college students or recent grads.

Amnesty International, San Francisco, CA
Volunteer Research Intern
- Conducted extensive research project on student activism, cited in Amnesty International's 2000 Annual Report.

- Designed questionnaires to survey university students, interviewed students, and collected data.

- Presented weekly progress reports to directors and members.

Community Outreach Project, Phoenix, AZ
Volunteer Youth Counselor
- Volunteered as a Big Brother three times a week for youth attending program in place of juvenile jail.

- Led discussions and counseling sessions once a week.

Department of Mental Health, Jacksonville, FL
Computer and Office Intern
- Co-directed a team of students in project performing employee skills assessments of computer and technology use.

- Interned with technology support team responding to employee needs.

Exploration Summer Programs, New Haven, CT
Youth Instructor
- Directed, planned, and managed daily activities, events, and discussions at enrichment program for 1,500 students.

Ross, Silverman & Levy LLP, Boston, MA
Legal Aide
- Assisted and supported attorneys on a variety of immigration cases, including business, family, and refugee immigration.

- Maintained firm's database with client financial information.

- Researched immigration legal issues, monitoring changes in immigration law post–September 11th.

Before

Retail Store Clerk
- Worked the register and helped customers at a hardware store.

After

Salesperson and Customer Service Representative
- Assisted customers with purchases, returns, exchanges, discount promotions, and equipment selection.
- Managed cash register, tracked financial transactions, and organized cash receipts in hardware store with weekly revenue of $100,000.

Rachel's Corner

The first time that I experienced the interviewer's end of the application process was in college. Partnered with an admissions officer, I interviewed my peers who were seeking positions as tour guides for the university. One girl really impressed me. She was well dressed, confident, funny, and knowledgeable about the school. When she left, I immediately said: "I like her; she's great." The admissions officer wrinkled her nose and responded, "Did you see her hair? It was soaking wet, as if she just got out of the shower. It's like she didn't even take this interview seriously enough to give herself time to dry her hair." I discovered at that moment how the most minute details can make or break an interview. And there I was, thinking she got extra points for showering.

Face/Off: Looks Matter

Well, the written version of you must've been impressive, because now they want to meet you in the flesh. Not to make you any more nervous than you are already, but the interview . . . well, if you screw it up, it's over. Jim, a guidance counselor in Boston, says, "If your employer doesn't feel like he can deal with your personality on a daily basis, he's not going to hire you." No pressure.

Forget everything your mom told you when you came home crying after the kids at school made fun of your fake Adidas sneakers. While "it's what's on the inside that counts" may have gotten you through some trying years of acne and awkwardness, in the real world, looks do matter.

Pauline, who has worked in voice communications for twenty years, says,

> Let's face it, chances are that most of the applicants come to the table with about the same qualifications, and what will set you apart from the others is the initial impression when you walk into the interview.

The good news is that unless you're applying to be a supermodel, you don't have to look like one. The type of physical appearance that we mean is the type that you can actually control.

What to wear: Even if your work environment would be business casual, it never hurts to wear a suit, unless you have been told not to. Your clothes should be ironed, your shirt tucked in, your shoes clean. Grooming: Hair should be worn neatly. Don't wear it so that it covers your face in any way. If you have a hairstyle that may not be considered "corporate" (long hair on a guy, braids, or dreads, for instance), pull it back and style it as subtly as possible.

Ladies, make-up and nails should be understated, as should any scent that you choose to wear. You almost want your appearance to be a nonfactor, not the thing that they remember most. If you leave the interview with the label of "the girl with the raccoon eyes who took a bath in cucumber melon body spray," don't expect a call back.

The Boy Scouts Were Right

If you have any psychic powers, the days before an interview would be a good time to employ them. Jim, our friendly high school guidance counselor, encourages us to take an activity from our drama club days—role playing. "Take advantage of any opportunity to do a mock interview and receive some feedback from a third party."

You should sit with your résumé in front of you and try to predict what the interviewer will ask you. If you've had particularly exciting experiences (for example, if you wrote about a year-long position helping refugees in a third-world country), chances are you'll be asked to elaborate.

If you possess some type of inadequacy for the position to which you're applying (for instance, if the job asks for technology expertise and you've had no formal training in computers), plan a defense for this in advance. Preparation is key.

Kendall, a financial analyst who obtained his undergraduate business degree in 1999, says,

> I actually design a couple of prepared statements before an interview that I can use as responses to several different types of questions. Like, interviewers always ask the "give an example of a problem and how you solved it" type question. So have your answer ready.

Interviewers always seem to ask applicants to describe a negative quality of theirs—almost a trick question. So think about

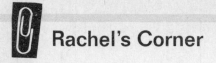

Rachel's Corner

In my high school, each student was required to participate in an activity called Declamation. Three times per year, we had to stand in front of our English class and recite a memorized speech or poem of substantial length. While it was torture at the time, since then I've realized how that mandatory activity prepared me for public speaking under all types of circumstances. When interviewing, you must speak loudly and clearly. Your energy and enthusiasm should come through your voice. You should look your interviewer directly in the eye. Eliminate all of those speech fillers such as "um," "like," and "you know." You may not earn an "A" on your report card, but you could earn yourself a paycheck.

ways to give certain negative qualities a positive spin, such as perfectionism, workaholism, or being uber-controlling. No matter what your response in an interview, always present answers in a positive light.

More than likely, as the interview is wrapping up, your potential employer will lean back in her chair and ask, "Now, do you have any questions for us?" It's always a good idea to ask at least one. The subliminal message of asking a final question is, "I'm still interested in working here! Hire me!" Just be careful: You don't want to ask a question that was already answered in the interview, or that you should've known before you even got there.

One strategy is to base your questions around the culture of the office, and the personal experiences of those who work there. Example: "What do young employees find to be the most challenging aspect of working here?" Or: "What opportunities exist for personal and professional development?"

Another tactic is showing your eagerness to learn more than you already do and demonstrating that you paid attention. Observe: "I'm intrigued by what you mentioned earlier regarding the relationship between the stock market and what you do here. Do you have any suggestions for where I could learn more about that?"

To Thine Own Self Be True

While interviews are all about putting your best foot forward, don't go in wearing someone else's shoes. If you try to be someone you're not, either they'll see through it or they'll hire the fake you and expect to see him or her show up to work every day. Don't pretend to have interests that you don't. You could get caught in a lie, which will immediately eliminate you from the pool of applicants. Ben, the Ohio architect with endless good advice, underscores the value of a positive attitude and interest level over experience:

> I believe that for most professions, your value right out of school is at least 80 percent attitude. Often it's much higher. Be energetic, be excited, and be yourself. Show them right away exactly what they're going to get if they hire you. If they ask you a question you don't know, explain that you're anxious to learn the answer.

Rachel's Corner

I was at the most important interview of my young life, competing for a grad school scholarship. It was going smoothly, but then one spoiler had to go and mess it all up. My interviewer asked me to expound on a current event linking three countries, which he then named (two of which I'd never heard of). I sat stupefied for a full minute. Finally, I told him the truth: I'd been so busy cramming for this interview that I'd lost touch with current events. And I told him that this was a shame, not because it was ruining my chances at getting the scholarship, but because I wanted to teach inner-city youth, and they'd be looking to me to inform them about society's problems. I got the scholarship, and I know now that it pays to be honest. But it also pays to watch the news.

Ellie, a retired health care executive, agrees with Ben's point about personality. Ellie has interviewed and hired numerous individuals throughout her career. Which is why she recommends the following: "Show flexibility of thought, enthusiasm, and a sense of humor. All else can be learned."

Lynn, a thirty-one-year-old teacher in Boston, decided to take the honest route when interviewing for her teaching position. The principal of the school, a very prim and proper woman, asked her what her favorite TV show was.

I was caught off-guard, because I didn't see that question coming. I wanted to say something like *Nightline* to sound worldly,

Crossfire: Typical Interview Questions

Q: What makes this position a good match for you?
(Watch out: This question can often wear various disguises. Common aliases are: "Why are you interested in this job?" and "Why are you the ideal candidate for this position?")

A: There are two ways to answer this question. If you're indeed applying for a job that matches your education and work history perfectly, then congratulations. There is no B.S. required for your response (and we're not talkin' 'bout no Bachelor of Science). Just briefly recap what you know about the position, and review the aspects of your background that prove your knowledge of specific job responsibilities. Observe:

I'm aware that the position requires me to organize several major fundraising events over the course of the year. My major was marketing and sales, and during college I was in charge of public relations for my business fraternity. We organized several charitable events each year, and I took the lead in planning those. I also assisted the woman who designed and implemented all fundraising efforts at my summer internship.

Now, in today's job market and in our general refusal to admit that there are limitations to our capabilities, we more often find ourselves applying for positions that are not exact matches at all. Here's where the B.S. comes in: Your job is to make your potential employer see something promising in you. Check this out:

While teaching sixth-grade science would be new to me, I'm totally prepared and excited about the challenge. I didn't major in science, but I did major in public health, which required a number of science courses. And while I haven't taught any academic classes, I have worked as a camp counselor for preteens for several years now. Twelve-year-old-speak is my second language. I know that teaching requires great public speaking skills, and I was on a prize-winning debate team in college. Presenting information in fun and innovative ways is also critical, and as a resident advisor for a freshman dorm, I had to devise interesting activities to educate the students on issues like time management, drugs, and health concerns.

Q: What is your best quality?
(a.k.a. "biggest strength" or "trait of which you're most proud")
   A: Choose a trait that has relevance to the position for which you're applying. Unless you're applying to be a bartender, mentioning that you make excellent cocktails probably isn't the way to go. Being a good communicator, innovative thinker, problem solver, or someone who works well under pressure are all useful characteristics in work settings. The trick is to support it with some specific evidence. In other words, attach it to a damn good story. Like this:

I'm a definite extrovert, and I think it works to my advantage. Even when I was younger, I never feared socializing with strangers or taking the initiative to lead a discussion. My senior year in high school, I had to go to a fancy dinner with a bunch of old, rich alumni. All of the other kids at my table were acting really shy and giving one-word answers every time one of the gruff old men asked them a question. I just acted like myself and asked them questions right back. A few months later, one of the men at that table gave me a college scholarship just from meeting me at that one dinner.

Q: What is your worst quality?
(a.k.a. "area of concern" or "characteristic that requires some work")

A: Yes, this is indeed a trick question. Any mention of laziness, flakiness, being overly sensitive, or having a hot temper will likely get your application placed in the trash. Here, you should find an honest fault in your character and make it sound almost like a strength. Traits such as perfectionism, extreme attention to detail, competitiveness, and the need for control are all "bad" qualities that can sound really good. Here's how a pro operates:

I have a difficult time relinquishing responsibility to others. Group projects were always difficult for me. I get along very well in groups, and I'll often facilitate when we have trouble coming to a consensus, but when it comes time to create a final product, I feel myself volunteering for most of the tasks. It's not because I don't trust my group mates, but I do like to take ownership for work that is going to bear my name.

Q: What is the accomplishment of which you're most proud?
(a.k.a. "obstacle you successfully overcame" or "your personal success story")

A: Here's the only time in your whole life where being born with a silver spoon and an easy ticket to ride is a bad thing. Nothing works better than the hard luck tale—we love to hear stories about people who pulled themselves up by their bootstraps. Near-death experiences are also fabulous. Unfortunately, most of us are quite ordinary. What we need to do is pull something interesting and admirable out of our otherwise dull existences. A quick list:

- Unusual travel experiences—any place where English is not the native language can be made into a tantalizing anecdote, especially if you traveled alone.

- Educational victory despite fairly overwhelming odds, but please don't ignore the "overwhelming odds" part. Graduating from college is not a feat in itself. A potential employer doesn't care that you went to 75 percent of your classes, even though some of them met early in the morning. Graduating from college *is* worth a pat on the back when you had to foot the entire bill yourself. When you suffered a family crisis during finals. When you have a learning disability. You get the idea.

- Landing yourself something cool through hard work and ingenuity: This could be the story of how you obtained an awesome internship or a competitive fellowship. Here's the rub: If you scored these sweet deals because your grandfather is on the selection committee, it's no longer a "great accomplishment."

A Few No-Nos

The term *overcoming obstacles* can sometimes throw young people off track. Obstacles for us are often things such as rocky romantic relationships, bad hair days, and a moderate addiction to beer. Personal stories that reveal aspects of you that should remain hidden from an employer are not the way to go.

Don't select a mundane incident as your greatest feat. For example, if being a camp counselor was your biggest challenge, you'd better have worked at Future Criminals of America. Well, maybe not that extreme, but you should at least be able to describe in detail a particularly difficult young person on whom you made an impact.

but I was scared she'd ask me some follow-up. So I went with the truth: *Buffy the Vampire Slayer*. I was hired, although they did give me the youngest grade in the school to teach.

Taboo Interview Topics

Read this very carefully:

1. **No dough.** Unless you're asked about salary needs, don't mention pay on a first interview. It's presumptuous, as you may not even be hired. You could also do yourself a disservice by stating a salary that is lower than what you may have been paid.

2. **Don't overshare.** Sometimes you'll encounter that magical interview in which you and your potential employer just completely vibe. You're chatting, laughing, completely comfortable. It's great that the interview is going so well, but don't ruin it by thinking that the two of you are closer than you really are. Don't talk about the night before when you got drunk at a bar, or how hot his secretary is. Things could quickly go from fun-loving to serious.

3. **Don't trash your last job.** Your interviewer is going to feel a sense of kinship to your last boss. It's not a good idea to make that last person look bad. The interviewer will most likely view you as the problem, not your boss.

4. **Avoid politics.** Your interviewer will likely have a political bent more liberal or conservative than your own. Un-

less your opinions about current events are integral to
the potential position, steer clear.

5. **No more drama.** Jim gives some guidance: "Your interview
should not include references to difficulties you've encountered unless these obstacles provide clear evidence of
your ability to deal with adversity. For example, if you've
struggled with depression, this is not the time to make a
full confession, even if you've made a complete recovery."

Remember Me?

The rules of follow-up after the application process is over
are similar to the rules after a first date. You definitely want
the other person to know you had a good time. In office culture, this is done in the form of a monetary bribe. Or, you can
write a thank-you letter. You're jobless, so let's choose the inexpensive approach.

Kelly, a research associate who is applying to business
school, gives a tip to making a thank-you note stand out:

> Try to include a detail or joke you talked about at your inter-
> view. And if the interviewer suggested that you research a cer-
> tain topic further, tell him or her what your findings have been
> since you last spoke.

Once you've done that, unless you've been asked to follow
up again, it's a waiting game. Just like you wouldn't call a
romantic interest if he or she never gave you their number,
you don't call someone at the office before the time that

they promised to get back to you. After that time has elapsed, make the call, and leave a detailed message if the person can't be reached, stating the position for which you applied and the date that you were supposed to have heard back.

Be polite and try not to sound too anxious.

Total Recall

- Carefully research each specific company or organization to which you're applying, or you could look like an idiot.

- Cover letters: Make them personalized, professional, and precise. Don't simply repeat the contents of your résumé. Instead, draw compelling connections between your experience and the requirements of the position for which you're applying.

- You want your resume to be polished, professional, well organized, and crafted in a way that maximizes your past jobs and experiences. Triple-check grammar, punctuation, and formatting. Forget to dot an "i" and you can forget obtaining an interview. Readability is key.

- When interviewing, a professional appearance counts. So does bathing. And preparedness is crucial. Anticipate questions and consider certain answers ahead of the interview. And remember to put on your most enthusiastic and energetic face.

- When interviewing, be honest while steering clear of unprofessional topics (such as salary discussions).

- Follow up after the interview with a personalized thank-you note. You'd be amazed at how much this gesture can help you stand out from other applicants.

4

Show Me the Money

(or accepting or declining a job offer)

Let's keep it real for a second here. Many of you might need to skip this chapter. If the bills are piling up and there are no other jobs in sight, then you probably don't have much to debate when a position is offered to you. Any paycheck is better than no paycheck, and if you're in dire financial straits, beggars can't be choosers.

However, you might find yourself lucky enough to be wanted in this tough job market. Good for you. In that case, you need to carefully consider your options and decide which job offer is the best one for you.

And what does "best" mean? Is it the highest salary, the most valuable experience, or the most enjoyable work environment? The answer? Yes.

- Money Matters
- 401 Que?
- Free Drugs, Almost
- Location Ramifications
- The *Friends* Factor
- Burning the Midnight Oil
- Does the Glass Ceiling Have Cracks?
- Know Your Boss
- Final Jeopardy

Money Matters

Anyone who's ever said that salary doesn't matter when considering a job is lying. A job must be able to support your lifestyle, but your lifestyle might have to adjust to your salary while you're climbing the career ladder.

When evaluating whether a job offer sounds workable in terms of pay, come up with a monthly budget for yourself. Expenses include rent (which ideally should not exceed 25 percent of your gross income), utilities, student loans, car-related expenditures, food, phone, credit-card debt, clothing, recreation, and entertainment. When you add these together, it should become clear how much money you actually need to live from month to month.

After you calculate your monthly total, figure out your monthly salary. Remember that the number given to you by your employer is completely misleading. By the time Uncle Sam and the gang ransack your pay stub, you'll be left with only a fraction of what you had originally (depending on your salary, you could be paying from 25 to 50 percent—yes, 50 percent!—in taxes). And remember that you don't only want enough money to cover your expenses—you need to make a bit more if you want to build your savings.

To help you work your budget, there's a simple worksheet on the next page. You're probably a pro at this, but hey, we're just making sure.

If your salary doesn't make the cut, it might be time to reduce your expenses. Do you live in a place that requires you to own a car, or can you use public transportation? Could you get a roommate to cut down on living expenses? Can you reduce or eliminate your credit-card debt?

No one wants to feel like a scrub, especially when you work hard every day, but that's part of the game. If you don't start modestly, then you won't make a very good success story in the future, now will you?

To get an idea about how your particular salary offer compares with average salaries for similar positions in your industry, check out www.salary.com, a comprehensive resource that provides national averages for salaries in numerous jobs, adjusted by location. For example, this website can tell you the difference between the average salary for an editorial assistant in New York City, Philadelphia, and on a national level. Very interesting stuff. And sometimes infuriating.

401 Que?

Once you've analyzed the heck out of your salary, it's time to consider benefits. In your past jobs, benefits may have

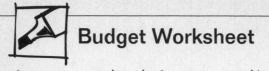

Budget Worksheet

As you get used to having money—yeah!—and spending money, having a budget and keeping track of your expenses can make your life much easier and your bank account fuller. You might be shocked to learn where your money goes—$60 on a bar tab?—and how quickly it goes. Reality check, here we come.

Monthly Income

Estimated take-home pay (salary – taxes – 401 [k] contribution)	
Money from family	
Money from investments	
TOTAL INCOME	

Monthly Expenses

Rent	
Utilities (heat, electricity, water)	
Telephone	
Cable TV and/or Internet	
Groceries	
Snacks or meals eaten out	
Transportation costs (car, bus, train, plane)	
Auto insurance (if applicable)	
Renter's insurance (if applicable)	

Student loans	
Medical bills/cost of medical or dental insurance	
Entertainment, recreation, and fitness	
Clothing	
Personal (haircuts, hygiene, health)	
TOTAL EXPENSES	
Net Income/Loss	
TOTAL INCOME–TOTAL EXPENSES	

 # Saving Moolah

Not many of us got through college without having to count our pennies, so you're probably a master at cutting corners. But just in case, here are a few ideas to get your frugal gene going and to save you a few bucks as you adjust to your life as a responsible and working adult. Right.

- Consider the "latte factor." Spending a few dollars a day on a latte and a muffin may seem inconsequential, but it can add up to more than $1,250 a year.

- Treat credit cards like debit cards by only spending money you actually have. If you end up carrying debt, use surplus savings to repay high-interest credit cards immediately.

- Determine which expenses are necessary versus needless. Take the time to compare prices on different options and prioritize where to spend your hard-earned dollars. Also, whenever possible, try to cut down on costs by sharing expenses with a friend, roommate, or partner.

- The importance of saving can be summed up in two words: compound interest. Research the best bank rates available and consider the relative risks and rewards of putting your money into interest-bearing checking accounts, mutual funds, or money-market accounts. Time is your ally.

- Being creative can save you a lot of money. Take advantage of your local library instead of always buying books or magazines. Think about the myriad activities you enjoy that are free or cost almost nothing, whether it's taking a walk, hitting the beach, renting a movie, or attending a book reading or a lecture.

- Check out these must-visit financial websites:

  www.fool.com
  www.moneycentral.com
  www.bankrate.com

included free pizza or discounted clothes. But in the "real world," benefits mean a lot more than that.

Marc, a twenty-seven-year-old development executive for a college in Maine, offers this advice:

Become knowledgeable about your benefits and pension plan—it's very easy to just sign whatever papers your human resources representative puts in front of you whenever it's time to select your benefit plan.

Many companies offer tax-deferred savings plans, such as a 401(k) or 403(b). Most employees will have a 401(k) plan, while employees of public schools and certain tax-exempt or religious organizations will have a 403(b) plan instead. The gist of both these plans involves taking pretax money out of your paycheck (GASP) to put into mutual fund investments for your retirement. Yes, it kind of sucks that you have to consider your life at sixty when you haven't even gotten your life at twenty-five together yet, but with social security's unsure future and the cost of living rising exponentially, you have to think about how you'll be livin' in your older (hmm, hmm, wiser) years.

A 401(k) or 403(b) is an extremely good thing because:

- Contributions are automatically deducted from your paycheck.
- It's one of the simplest ways to save for retirement.
- Your contributions are pretax—this means that you're actually taxed on a lower amount of money. A good thing.
- Companies often match employee contributions.
- 401(k) funds are unaffected if you change employers.
- 401(k) funds are not taxed until you take them out.

We don't claim to be financial wizards, so to learn more details about 401(k) and 403(b) plans, spend some time on the Motley Fool website: www.fool.com. There isn't another site as down-to-earth and comprehensive regarding matters of personal finance.

Free Drugs, Almost

On another bright note, what if you get sick? Health plans require serious consideration. Many jobs offer plans where you pay a nominal fee each pay period (GASP Part II) and the company pays the bulk of your health insurance costs. Plans usually include free yearly physicals, reduced-cost prescriptions, and emergency room care. You're also often entitled to mental health treatment, and some health plans even offer reduced gym membership.

The dental benefits generally consist of a free cleaning or two per year, but if you're getting a lot more than that, you clearly work for a company with a great benefits package. Extra points for them.

 ## Rachel's Corner

I am a teacher for the Boston Public Schools, and while you've probably heard that teachers make jack smack (which is, well, true), we do get great benefits. Take advantage of the few good things you're offered in a position, because even if you move to a job that pays more, you might lose out on some of the other bonuses. For example, I can get new glasses every two years. So I do. We get two free teeth cleanings per year. So I go. We even get breaks on property down payments. Therefore, a lot of my young colleagues are buying houses.

Learn about all the extras that your job has to offer, and make them work for you.

Vision coverage depends on the employer, but you should by no means expect help from your employer with eyewear and vision appointments. Blindness, here we come.

The costs of health insurance are rising, and some companies are cutting benefits and requiring employees to contribute a greater portion of their health insurance costs. Make sure that you understand exactly what your job offer includes in terms of health insurance and how much you'll have to pay versus how much your employer will be picking up.

Website www.fool.com is to personal finance questions what www.insure.com is to insurance questions. Easy to understand and exhaustively thorough. Check it out.

Location Ramifications

Your job predicament is made ten times more complicated when it involves a geographical move. There are two possible situations:

1. You wanted to go someplace new, so you found jobs in that area.
2. You found the perfect job for you, but it requires you to make a residential change.

If you fall into the first category, make sure that you're not accepting the job just because it's in a great place to live. Anything in Miami sounds appealing when you live in New Hampshire, but if you don't like your job, Miami may lose some of its appeal.

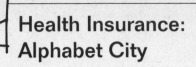

Health Insurance: Alphabet City

Health insurance varies from employer to employer, but it's a benefit of full-time employment that you'll come to love and hate. We love it because we need it, because with it we feel protected and safe, and because it saves us tons of money on health care. We hate it because health insurance is bureaucratic, because it's full of restrictions on coverage, and because it's very expensive for individuals without help from an employer. Here's some basic lingo you should know:

PCP: Primary Care Physician

Most plans require that you select a PCP who becomes your primary point of contact. You can access specialists, if necessary, through referrals from your PCP.

HMO: Health Maintenance Organization

HMOs are the least expensive health care plan, but they're also the least flexible. In an HMO, you must select a PCP within the HMO network, unless you want to pay for the care yourself. Small price to pay, considering that HMOs greatly reduce copayments for care and involve minimal paperwork.

PPO: Preferred Provider Organization

A PPO plan differs from an HMO plan because participants aren't obligated to select a PCP. This means that members are actually allowed to see specialists without a referral from a PCP. Problem is, you have to ante up a higher copayment for that freedom. PPOs make it cheaper to follow their rules (staying within the network), but they do allow members to pay a higher copay for flexibility (going outside the network).

POS: Point of Service

A POS plan is the middle ground between HMOs and PPOs. While you must select a PCP, you're allowed to visit doctors and specialists outside the network with permission from your PCP. As you may have guessed, you pay more to leave the POS network.

If you're on the opposite end of the spectrum and want the job but don't want the move, you have some serious thinking to do. Nkechi, a twenty-six-year-old trader for the Federal Reserve Board, says, "If a company really wants you and you're hesitant to move, the least they can do is include some additional incentives, like covering some of your moving costs." Perhaps the job offer was just what you needed to get out of your comfort zone. Or you might decide that the perfect job just has to find its way to *you*, and not the other way around.

The *Friends* Factor

You'll spend more hours at work than you do in your own bedroom. So it's important to enjoy your working environment at least somewhat. Think back to your on-site interviews. When you were introduced to your coworkers, did they appear interested? When watching people in their own work setting, did you notice smiles or growls? Do these people seem to get along? Are there any social activities through work?

Rachel's Corner

One summer during college, I had to choose between two jobs: one on campus in Philadelphia and the other at home in Boston. Spending the warm months with my friends on campus sounded great. However, I appealed to my practical side and went with the summer at home. First, the pay was much better at the job in Boston. The reduced expenses of living at home also made it a hard deal to pass over. Second, while both were secretarial jobs, the Boston position was at a prestigious design firm; the one in Philly was for my school's dining services. Lastly, I tried to be rational about the social benefits. I wouldn't be miserable at home because I still had my friends from high school in Boston. We ultimately had a cool summer and I returned to campus with fatter pockets, all the better to enjoy the fall semester.

Jenee, a high school teacher for the past five years, says:

One of my favorite moments from my early years of teaching was when the teachers organized to form a softball team that played against the students. It was so great seeing people whom you normally only know in "serious" mode goofing around and having fun. I feel like it created a bond that lasted even after we lost miserably.

A job is a job, and you don't have to be best friends with your coworkers. But if you have several job offers, a better working atmosphere might just break the tie.

Apartment Dreams

Haven't we all fantasized about having our own place? The idea of all our friends chillin' at the spot, their feet on the coffee table, and no one to yell at them—it doesn't get any better. Add on the hours that we've spent watching *MTV Cribs*, and we've got ourselves a downright unattainable fantasy.

When we envision our first apartment, we picture the few times a year that we'll actually take full advantage of the social benefits of living independently. We don't think about the many times per month that we write checks for housing-related bills—rent, heat, water, electricity, cable, phone, and Internet, just to name a few. Don't forget the start-up money required to *get* an apartment. Often you'll need the first and last month's rent, as well as a security deposit. In certain cities, there are also finder's fees—a month's rent paid to the real estate agent that gets you the place. Worst-case scenario is having to pay four months of rent up front.

Therefore, it's essential that you think of ways to cut costs. First off, must you live alone? Think of all the TV shows that revolve around roommates: *The Real World*, *Will & Grace*, *Friends* . . . clearly there's an appeal. And aside from all of the laughs and random hookups that those television programs highlight, living with one or more people dramatically reduces expenses.

It's also time to prioritize—while you might have thought that cable TV was a necessity when you lived with your parents, it's now time to weigh your options. Cable . . . or heat? You decide. Watching *Six Feet Under* in subzero-degree temperatures is a little too close to reality television for most of us.

And if you decide that you need all of the trappings of super-salary life, it's time to do the unthinkable: Live at home. Yes, that's right. With mom, dad, grandma, or any family member who is willing to house your sorry butt for little-to-no money. Yes, your dreams of wild parties are over. But at least you'll be able to afford an outfit to wear to someone else's.

Burning the Midnight Oil

Softball team or not, unless you're a complete freak, you don't want to spend *all* of your time at work. So, how much actual time does this job require?

Nadine, a first-year lawyer in Boston, wasn't ready for the time commitment during her first year at a law firm.

I was really excited when I learned what my salary would be. Then I started coming home from work at 10:00 and 11:00 at night, sometimes even later. Since I couldn't earn overtime, I realized why I was being paid so well.

Nadine says that knowing her hours still wouldn't have changed her decision to become a lawyer with her firm, but maybe you're not ready to put in that level of commitment. It's fair to ask your employer how much overtime is necessary or expected in your job position.

Ben, that seminude architect from Ohio, adds,

Overtime can make a huge difference. If you're working at a job where you'll undoubtedly work many fifty- or sixty-hour weeks, overtime pay can increase your yearly salary by up to $10,000. Do the math.

Food

Living on your own is the best way to either gain a ton of weight or waste away to nothing. The excess fat comes in when you eat all of your meals at the fast-food place on the corner. The incredible shrinking occurs if you don't eat, since you can't cook.

If you're reading in anticipation of a magic solution that's going to allow you to eat healthy, economical meals without ever having to turn on a stove, you'll be disappointed. The first rule when it comes to food is that you're going to have to learn to make some. Good news—some of the easiest things to cook are also the cheapest. Pasta is a great example.

When buying groceries, don't turn up your nose at generic brands. If you're averse to putting a plain, white box of cereal with black writing in your cart, buy the supermarket's signature brand. It's a little less bootleg. And since no one our age spends Sunday afternoons cutting coupons, get a discount card from your supermarket instead. Each week there are sales on certain items for people with the magic card (and yes, the card is free). Wait to buy treats until they're on sale.

When eating out at fancy restaurants (i.e., not McDonald's), order something that makes a good doggie bag. And if someone else is paying, get the largest meal on the menu. Not the most expensive, but the one that piles the largest amount of food on the plate. You could be set for the next few days, as long as you have a microwave and a set of Tupperware.

Don't forget the kissing cousin to food—drink. If you enjoy the partaking of beverages of an alcoholic nature, the liquor store is a better bargain than the bar. Keeping a bar at your own house not only makes you super cool and grown-up-like, but it saves you from emptying your wallet when you go out at night.

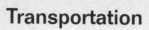

Transportation

Watch any car commercial and you'll see why cars are so integral to being an American: cars = freedom. Yet people often forget the other reason cars represent America so well: cars = debt. Cars are expensive, and as you head out into the wide blue yonder sans parents, it's important to carefully consider your transportation options.

- Compare your options. Is there public transportation for your workday commute? Would you only use the car on weekends? How often would you drive?

- Each year, *Consumer Reports* publishes an annual summary of key product ratings, covering dishwashers to digital cameras to cars, SUVs, and trucks. Take a peek—it's an excellent way to begin your car research.

- View prices in your area on specific vehicle models and years by visiting sites like www.cars.com or www.autotrader.com.

- Remember that car-related expenses are significant. Calculate monthly insurance, gas, and maintenance. Bottom line: Don't spend the maximum you can afford on the car alone. Routine (or unexpected) repairs can be substantial.

- Is a car necessary, or is it a luxury? Be honest with yourself. No, seriously.

To get a better idea of what your hours might be like, see if you can talk to the people who work at the company. The person making you the offer may not want to tell you that you'll never see sunlight again once you start your job.

Does the Glass Ceiling Have Cracks?

Perhaps this job is merely a pit stop until the economy turns right side up, or until you figure out what you really want to do with your life. But unless you're sure that you want nothing out of your company besides a paycheck, you must consider the long-term possibilities.

As if you don't have enough to think about when choosing whether you want this position, it's critical to consider the potential for growth. Take note of what your employer indicated regarding opportunities for advancement. Does he or she seem interested in your future goals? Are there other employees at the company who started in one place and through hard work reached a better place?

Keira, a twenty-something entrepreneur in New York, suggests: "Find out if there's opportunity for you to grow as a professional. Are there opportunities to be involved in things that will give you valuable experience?" For example, Is there tuition reimbursement for graduate school? Are there workshops and mini-courses offered through the company? and Do they assign mentors to new employees?

Know Your Boss

Your boss can turn your great job into a miserable one, or vice versa. There isn't much you can do about choosing who your boss will be, but if you have a few job offers on your hands,

Ari's Corner

During college, I began doing literary research for a boss who was in the process of writing a book. He not only valued my input, but he mentored me in a way that increased my confidence and skills. Three years later, I returned to work as a consultant for his newly formed company. Later on, a different boss was kind enough, but she never expressed an interest in mentoring me. Perhaps because of my age, she gave more challenging tasks to others in the organization. It wasn't long before I felt disconnected from the job. My experience has taught me that it's crucial to find a boss who cares not just about what you produce but also about helping you grow and making you feel like a valued member of the team.

the quality of your future boss must figure into your decision about which offer to accept.

Here's some good advice from Peter, who is the former president of a foundation and most recently was the publisher of an international newspaper. Over the past few decades, he has counseled and mentored hundreds of up-and-coming colleagues.

The most important thing for a young person in an early job is the quality of the boss, not the field of the job. Find someone who is a sharer, who is curious, who is generous, who is wise, who is ethical, who takes joy in watching able juniors grow, blossom, and eventually surpass him or her.

Do research on your potential boss. Most people think interviewing and evaluating is what the hirer should do. Wrong. The hiree should do it, too. You ought to be able to fill five pages of thoughtful, penetrating, and fairly comprehensive views and information about anyone you would consider trusting to be your boss before you make the decision.

Final Jeopardy

So you grin, nod, and shake hands, ready to embark on the journey into the working world. If you have any choice over your start date, consider making your first week a short one. Starting on a Wednesday or Thursday gives you some time to adjust without being exhausted by five straight days of new information.

If you decide that you and the job just aren't a match, there is a wrong and a right way to say no. Nabulungi, our wise executive assistant in Los Angeles, says,

> Be gracious about declining an offer so that they'll continue to think of you if another opportunity comes your way. Don't simply fail to reply as a means of letting them know that you're not interested.

You don't have to feel obligated to share the details of why you're choosing one job offer over another. It's okay to simply say that you're going to pursue another opportunity. At the same time, there might be value in revealing why you're heading in a different direction. For example, if the other job offer comes with a higher salary, you may politely mention it in the hopes that your other potential employer loves you so much that they'll want to match it.

Terrance, a network engineer in Virginia for the past two years, encourages candor: "You never know when your honesty might lead to a better offer package."

Total Recall

- Salary: Do your research. Do you have a minimum figure in mind? Have you figured out your monthly budget? Have you checked out www.salary.com?

- Have you considered the nonsalary benefits or perks of a job? Does the company provide good health care coverage or maybe a discount gym membership?

- Will you have friends or family where you're working? How easy will the daily commute be? Will you be making any sacrifices professionally or socially?

- What are your impressions of your potential colleagues and the office atmosphere? Do people have lunch together, by themselves, or not at all? How well did you get along with your interviewers?

- What kind of expectations will the company have of you regarding work schedule? What kind of a commitment are you willing to make?

- What do you think of your potential new boss as a supervisor and mentor? Will this person help you develop personally and professionally? Could you see yourself working for this person happily?

- If turning down an offer, be honest yet tactful. There's no reason to burn bridges. There can also be benefits to sharing why an offer doesn't appeal to you, since this can result in a better offer.

5

It's Not Easy Being Green

(or settling into a new position)

The good news is that somehow you've been hired. It's your first day on the job, you're excited, and you want to make a difference. But you have no idea about prioritizing tasks, you're not sure how often to check in with your boss, and you don't know where the bathroom is.

First, locate the restrooms—that's life or death. Second, prepare yourself to absorb a tsunami of information. From meetings with your boss and colleagues, to discerning the ways of your office environment, to conveying the right attitude from the start, there's a lot to handle in your first few weeks and months on the job.

So read on for some suggestions on how to get through this tricky time with flying colors.

Memorize This Advice

Denise is a director of human resources. This means she hires people just like you. (She also fires them.) So listen up, because it's your hide on the line.

Step One: Chat with the Chief

"Be sure you establish a way of communicating with your supervisor that works for both of you. Ask what she prefers and be sure to get into the mix what works best for you. You may have to take the lead on this, believe it or not.

"Set up regular meetings with your supervisor in the early months of your employment. And take advantage of that time by being prepared with questions—you need to be clear about what you feel you'll need from your new supervisor. Be sure to let her know what conditions make it possible for you to be your most productive. A good supervisor will work toward your strengths."

Step Two: Open Your Eyes

"Get a lay of the land. It's rare that the picture painted about an organization when you interview is totally accurate—just like an applicant, companies and organizations focus on the positive and minimize the negative."

Step Three: Emulate the Stars

"Get to know the top performers in the organization and determine what it is that they do, why the company cares about what they do, and what skills or knowledge they have that's highly valued by the organization. Then, to the extent possible, do what these top performers do."

Step Four: Identify the, Um, Nonstars

"Avoid the nay-sayers as you enter an organization, and the marginal performers—at least initially. Later you may come to understand why they feel the way they do. Some of their reasoning may have merit, but starting off hanging with the negative crowd is not wise."

Yes, Your Majesty

If your supervisor hasn't arranged an initial meeting to delineate what's expected of you, then set that up immediately. Aya, a research analyst a few years out of grad school, breaks it down: "Ask your supervisor and coworkers what

We Talk With . . .
Ellie, Nonprofit Program Assistant

What are your top priorities when settling into a new position?
Having only settled into a job once, I can comment on what I'd do differently next time. First and foremost, if at all possible, talk to your predecessor and ask tons of questions: Where they put their files, where things are on the computer, is there a job manual, and so on. Ask him or her about the most important part of your job and which priorities are critical to your supervisor. Ask what parts are the toughest and which take the most time, but ask questions.

Try to understand the organization and all the different components really well. Read the website inside and out and make sure that you know all the different parts—soon you'll realize that you understand what your responsibilities are and what are the top priorities for the organization.

What questions or topics are important to address with your supervisor?
Ask many questions and find out how your supervisor thinks about things, whether he or she's a big-picture thinker or whether they like the details right away. Set up a time to meet to have built-in reflection time—an hour or so a week to go over what you're working on. Yes, you'll likely talk to your boss all the time about little topics, but a scheduled time to reflect on the work you've done and how it can be improved upon will give you a sense of accomplishment as well as invaluable personal development.

Also, ask logistical questions: Can you use your work email for personal use? How does your company feel about your receiving minimal but some personal phone calls? What hours should you work? Is there a certain dress code?

they expect of you—that way you won't be surprised later if you get into 'trouble' and cause misunderstandings."

Consider a discussion of expectations as an opportunity not only to learn what your boss wants from you but also as a chance to discuss what you hope to accomplish in the coming months. There's nothing more effective than establishing clear objectives, which can be later measured and assessed (that's how you get a raise, Smarty Pants).

Ed manages a loan fund, and he advises:

Whenever you start a new job, it's very important to list the goals you want to accomplish and share them with your supervisor. This task is not always the most fun, and it can be difficult to state what goals you want to reach when you may not even be sure of what your job entails. However, this step is instrumental in building political capital within your organization if you reach your goals and will position you in an excellent place for advancement.

Ben's Corner

To the extent possible, I've set concrete, quantifiable goals for my positions in the past with my supervisors. I've typically begun with fairly achievable objectives for my first couple of months, since first impressions do matter. I'd always rather exceed expectations than disappoint colleagues.

Also remember that it's much more powerful to boast about what you want to do and then quite modestly tell people that you reached your goals, rather than not saying anything initially and then boasting about your accomplishments after the fact. In the latter scenario, people may think you're a braggart and that you might be more lucky than good at your job. In the former scenario, people are more likely to think of you as an achiever.

Culture Club

In addition to clarifying your boss's expectations and your own professional goals, it behooves you to know your new work culture cold. If only the pressures of fitting in disappeared once we graduated from high school. But they don't, and some would argue that your ability to assimilate into your office culture is a principal determinant of your future success. Yikes. Sounds kind of heavy.

Bottom line, keep your eyes and ears open. Notice how people get things done, how your colleagues dress and behave, and even how people decorate their workspaces. It might sound silly, but whether or not you take your lunch at your desk can matter. Hopefully it won't—but do pay attention.

Karen is a controller, which means she runs an entire accounting department, and she recommends that new hires do the following:

Pay attention to the protocols of your work environment, such as whether it's acceptable to show up at someone's door to discuss something or if you need to set up a meeting in advance.

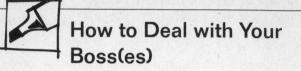

How to Deal with Your Boss(es)

Chances are that your first gig out of college isn't going to be as CEO. Therefore, it's time to learn how to get along with your boss, no matter what his or her personality type. Notice the term *get along* as opposed to "like" or "make friends with." Here are some tips for successful interactions with some of the more common types of supervisors.

Controlling, Micromanaging Boss

- Pay close attention to the types of details that are important to your boss, and try to find patterns and commonalities. That way, you can anticipate nit-picking before it happens. Anticipate, anticipate, anticipate.

- Don't brush off minute requests. If you complete them in a careful and timely manner, perhaps with time, he or she will trust that you won't need your boss hovering over your shoulder. Prove that you deserve his or her confidence.

Super-Busy, Absentee Boss

- First off, congratulations—you might've lucked out. Just ask the person with the omnipresent boss (see above).

- Create work plans that outline tasks and goals for the next week or month, and review the plan with your boss periodically.

- Find a second-in-command with whom you can consult if your boss isn't available.

Cold, Distant Boss

- Always interact in a cordial manner, but don't try to kill with kindness. People who are naturally icy aren't necessarily fans of sugar-sweet personalities.

- You could try to find topics that excite your boss and use those as ice-breakers. But it might work just as well to do your job and stay out of his or her way.

- Some people warm up with time. (It's the concept of thawing.) There's a chance that your supervisor's outward attitude toward you will improve. But if it doesn't, don't take it personally.

Stressed, Frazzled, Workaholic Boss

- Maintain a calm demeanor. Two high-strung people in the office are worse than one.

- This type of boss might be reluctant to assign tasks to others, out of fear that the job won't be completed to his or her satisfaction. Develop trust by volunteering to help whenever possible and by running the carefully reviewed finished product by him or her.

- Clearly define your supervisor's expectations of you. Depending on the position or specific projects, you may have to match their stressed, workaholic schedule and demeanor. (Not what you wanted to hear, was it?)

The Hands-Off, Laid-Back Boss (a.k.a. the Cool Boss)

- While this may seem like a dream come true, don't abuse it. Remember that this person still holds your fate in his hands and that you need to respect your professional relationship. In other words, a trip to the Strip Club with the Big Guy is not the best idea.

- Take initiative and be aggressive when it comes to defining your role in the workplace. Suggest objectives, plans, and ideas and elicit his buy-in. No matter how "cool" your boss is, he'll still demand solid goal setting and concrete, timely deliverables.

Ben's Corner

As a rule, my first week on the job, I don't bring lunch from home. Instead, I go out for lunch with colleagues. This is key for both building relationships and getting an insider's view on the company. It's also helpful for me to learn which Chinese place will give me the runs—something that's good to know ahead of time.

Karen's tip touches on an important task: figuring out how best to communicate with specific coworkers. You'll soon find that some respond better to email or voicemail or being caught in the hallway.

Young Blood

Looking like you're still a teenager isn't just annoying when you're out on the town and the bouncers keep carding you. It can also be a problem in the workplace. But have no fear—there are ways to use your age to your advantage.

Issue

It's difficult to command respect when I look like I just stepped out of a Clearasil commercial.

Solution

The way you present yourself has a huge impact on the way you're perceived. Make an extra effort to make your wardrobe completely professional.

Dudes:
While the older men at the office might get away with jeans and a blazer, err on the side of formality.

Ladies:
There's a difference between fitted pants and hot pants. The outfit you wore to the club cannot be "dressed up" for work.

Also, in the words of your admonishing mom, watch your mouth. No cursing and lighten up on the slang. Your language should not be much different from that of your colleagues.

Finally, do your job and do it well. If you prove yourself to be a reliable employee who takes responsibilities seriously, people will have no choice but to respect you.

Issue

I have a smaller knowledge base and much less life and work experience than my older colleagues.

Solution

Construct a fictional wife/husband and kids so you appear more versed in real life. Or not. Instead, take advantage of any and all professional development opportunities that your job offers. Seek the expertise of your colleagues and collaborate with them whenever possible. In short, display a willingness to widen your scope of knowledge, and it will be greatly appreciated.

Issue

As a fresh-faced, low man on the totem pole, I'm often given mundane tasks that are neither interesting nor challenging.

Solution

Assignments such as data entry, running errands, and taking phone calls could provide you with a more clear understanding of the way your company works. As you advance in your workplace, it's important to comprehend the organization from the bottom up.

There's a second piece of good news: Easy tasks are fabulous opportunities to do a kickass job. Instead of rushing through the irritating assignment of filing, create a filing system that will dazzle the higher-ups. When the tasks get harder, it won't be as easy to impress your superiors.

Issue

As the newest recruit, I get the smallest paycheck.

Solution

Since you have fewer expenses than a middle-aged homeowner putting his kids through college, it makes sense that you earn less. And there's nowhere to go but up when you're making pennies.

The Advantages of Being Young (Yes, There *Are* Some!)

- Employers will love your energy and motivation. While employees who've been on the job for several years will be complaining of burnout, your engine is just getting revved up.
- You can offer a fresh perspective to a team or project. Who better to come up with a new marketing strategy for the younger demographic? Who can tell a boss about an organizational technique that worked really well at a previous internship? You, silly rabbit.
- They can work you like a dog and not feel guilty. Younger people tend to have fewer personal commitments that take them away from work. When your colleagues have to leave early because a babysitter has canceled, you can call your friends and tell them you'll be a few hours late to the *Road Rules* marathon. This opens the door to first consideration for exciting business trips or wonderful relocation opportunities.
- As the newest recruit, you get the smallest paycheck. No, this is not a typo. While barely earning enough to make ends meet is not ideal for you, it *is* ideal for your company. In this age of budget cuts and financial crises, you might find yourself surviving a layoff before the senior member of your office. Why? Not because they think you're cuter. It's because they can afford you.

Shut Yer Yap

As is the case for most people, your colleagues want to feel like their voice matters. So let them talk. By listening to them, you can learn while strengthening relationships. We some-times forget that we can win the trust of many more people by hearing their ideas and caring about what they have to say than by trying to show them how much we know. Yes, we must be competent and vocal, but listening will take us a long way in those first few weeks on the job.

Mick, a veteran career coach, believes good listening cre-ates a lasting impact.

> Listen long before you act or speak. Total understanding of the dynamics of each situation, the levels of potential problems, and personality issues will allow your actions and words to be chosen so they're more likely to be received positively.

Sorry, I'm New Here

It's a good idea to listen, but you've got to speak up and ask a lot of questions when you start a new job. Lots of questions—because you're not perceived as "new" forever. Nabulungi, the executive assistant you've met before, underscores this point:

> Try to become really knowledgeable about your job responsi-bilities within the first couple of weeks and don't be afraid to

ask questions. It's much more embarrassing to ask a question three months into a job that you could've asked when you were still considered "new." Mistakes are much more likely to be acceptable as a rookie.

It also doesn't hurt to figure out the company's helpful cast of characters early on. Terrance, that IT engineer from chapter 4, offers this suggestion:

Get to know the people who really make things happen. When your computer crashes, phone doesn't work, or you need supplies, where do you go? It most likely isn't to your boss.

Attitude, Shmattitude

Truly excelling at work requires exceeding the expectations for your position. Building a reputation as a reliable, capable, and motivated coworker relates directly to your efforts to increase your responsibilities, get promoted, and get a raise.

MaryBeth is a twenty-nine-year-old probation officer in Maryland who offers this reality check:

When starting a new position, it's important to remember that you're earning a reputation, not a grade. Consistency is crucial, and cramming at the end is no longer an option. Arrive early, stay late, volunteer for challenging work, and ask questions.

We Talk With . . .
Gabe, Legal Assistant

How do you acclimate yourself to the office or company culture?
Any postgrad who's put in a few years in the working world will
tell you that from day one, you have to start building a positive
reputation among your supervisors and colleagues. This reputation can follow you until week 100. The key is to realize that
you're your own PR firm.

On a daily basis, you need to actively manage your reputation around the office. One way you can start off on the right
foot is by becoming a "go-to" guy or gal for special tasks and
topics around the office. For example, let your boss know in advance that you'd like a shot at a certain project the next time it
comes around. Or, without bragging, let your supervisor know
that you studied business in college or that you've taken a couple years of French or Japanese. After a while of taking on
these special responsibilities or projects, you may find yourself
as the first person your supervisor looks to when a new or challenging project comes along.

What should a person not do when first settling in?
When you're the new guy or gal, one of your top priorities should
be approaching the office relationships really slowly. Tread lightly
in this area. This may sound like common sense, but after a few
slipups, you may find that those stories you told to your new pals
over a coffee break somehow found themselves into an office
meeting . . . and everyone is looking at you just a little bit differently. So think and act humbly—don't brag, and whatever you
do, save the Monday-morning stories (especially any that include
references to college-related activities) for later down the road.

We Talk With . . .

Joe, Alumni Director for a
Youth Organization

What are important steps when starting a new position?
It's important to keep your eye on the goals and objectives of
your position. Whenever possible, get these goals defined in a
quantitative, measurable form. Then seek out the benchmarks
you'll need to accomplish these goals. Most positions will have a
track record from previous people who held that particular job,
and some detailed analysis will yield the benchmarks you'll need.

What should be discussed or defined with a supervisor?
In keeping focused on goals, be sure that your supervisor is
aware of your plan to reach the benchmarks you've set for
yourself. Also be open to his or her advice on a regular basis.
It's not to your advantage to have a supervisor who doesn't say
anything about your progress. No news is not good news. Ask
for advice. Be sure you're on track.

How should a person adjust to the office culture?
Most companies have a tone that you'll pick up from the first interview you have with the managers. Initially play off of this
tone, but don't feel you've mastered the company culture simply because you're getting along well the first few weeks or
even months. There's much more to an office culture than
meets the eye, and it can take a while to fully appreciate the
flow of a workplace.

What should a person not do when settling in?
Assume nothing. Instead, ask for clarification and review your
plan of action to fulfill the assignment with your supervisor.
Most good managers would say the only stupid question is the
one you didn't ask before moving ahead with an assignment.

Total Recall

- Find time to meet with your boss to define both your and his or her expectations and quantifiable goals for your position. Make sure that you and your supervisor are on the same page from day one.

- Identify positive colleagues with whom to associate initially. One of the quickest ways to excel is to model yourself after those who already have.

- Play the active observer role in perceiving office culture. What makes the office tick? Do colleagues hang out after work? What do people do for lunch? How is taking a break viewed?

- Use your youth to your advantage, making your age an asset. What young hires often bring to the table are fresh perspective, aggressive learning curve, flexible schedule, lower pay scale, energy, and ambition.

- Ask questions while it's still acceptable and expected of you, because you're not the new hire forever. The stupid question is the question unasked—until you've already been there three months and should've known what you were just asking about.

- Attitude matters. Almost more than anything else. Have a positive one and maintain it consistently. Realize that you're building a reputation that starts with first impressions and continues as long as you work at the company.

6

R-E-S-P-E-C-T

(or excelling in your position)

Excelling in the workplace can be tricky. If we lived in a perfect world, filled with apple pies and gold stars, representing ourselves at work could be much more simple and straight-forward. True merit and effort would be rewarded with raises and promotions, and sacrifice and dedication would be generously recognized and acknowledged. But to get where we're headed—endless career success and riches, of course—we have to champion our own causes, record and publicize our accomplishments, and direct our own professional development. It's doable, but it takes work.

If only Aretha could accompany us to work each day, singing our praises and demanding the respect we deserve.

- Marketing the Brand "You"
- Walk the Talk

- Think Swiss Army Knife
- Dog-Ear this Page
- Sitting at the Grown-Up Table
- Head of the Class
- Look in the Mirror, Quick
- (Im) Balance

Marketing the Brand "You"

Imagine that you're a brand, and that the brand's successes, failures, perception, reputation, and growth are in your hands. What must you do each day, week, and month to advance genuine brand awareness, confidence, appreciation, and development?

Charlotte, a director of communications, advises that individuals manage their own public relations, so to speak, and she stresses the importance of representing yourself and what you achieve, since no one else will.

Perception is reality. It doesn't matter if you're not the smartest or the most qualified for the position. What's most important is that you're *perceived* to be the smartest or the most qualified. We all know the person in the office who works very hard but is always overlooked for promotions or raises.

Don't be that person. If you want to get promoted, you should behave as if you already have the responsibilities of that position. If you want to get a big raise, you should show your employer why you deserve that raise. Don't be afraid to highlight your accomplishments, but don't embellish or lie—just

Ben's Corner

People make judgments based on what they see, and I've experienced this firsthand. Which means it's crucial to manage three specific aspects of your work persona: your clothing, your desk, and your hours. I wish I were kidding. But here it is, plain and simple: I dress professionally, I keep an organized and clean workspace, and I put in extra hours. Appearance counts more than you could ever imagine.

make sure that everyone in a position of power is aware of your capabilities and potential.

Maria, another experienced specialist in the public relations field, encourages positive yet restrained self-promotion:

You need to market yourself and make sure that those above you know the good, high-quality work you're producing or the solid relationships you're building with key clients. There's a subtle balance between coming off as if you're boasting and sharing the information in an appropriate context.

Remember that you need to first prove yourself and your work to your manager, who can then back you up when needed. Sometimes you'll get lucky and have a manager who'll keep more senior staff apprised of your work, but this isn't something you should count on.

I've found that sharing my successes with senior management has helped to inspire their confidence and trust in me.

Down the line, as you look to move forward in your career, it can also help to have recommendations from senior staff who really had the opportunity to know you, so they can give a genuine, positive recommendation to a potential new employer.

Walk the Talk

Charlotte and Maria have emphasized the importance of monitoring how you're perceived within your organization because, bottom line, your reputation matters.

But equally as essential is the actual work you get done. You can listen well, be considerate, and build strong relationships, but if you don't "deliver the goods," your employment will be short-lived. We all know the person in our workplace that talks a good game, drawing attention to even minor accomplishments. But we also know that bosses and colleagues eventually see through this facade.

Terry, a seasoned teacher, puts it simply: "Actions speak louder than words. People will be more successful if they let their work do their talking for them. Doing what's expected and beyond is how you advance." Just as in college, it's crucial to meet deadlines. But while you may be recognized for the speed with which you complete tasks or your willingness to put in long hours, in the end you'll be evaluated and recognized for the quality of your efforts. It's vital to produce high-caliber work in a short window of time. All that college training, here we come.

Ben's Corner

Master the technologies or tasks that others shun. Sounds silly, right? When I begin any position, I immediately focus on figuring out the daunting database, the security alarm system, the telephones and voice mail, conference calling, our UPS and FedEx accounts, the postage machine, and our printers and copiers. Seemingly low-level and administrative stuff. Yet it's why many times I was deemed the go-to guy from the first week, and it's why people viewed me as essential.

Think Swiss Army Knife

While everyone eventually finds a niche, being a jack-of-all-trades pays dividends. One of the best ways to find your place in an organization is by becoming aware and knowledgeable of all the roles people play. The more versatile you are, the more of an asset you'll be to your employers.

Now, this doesn't mean that you always have to pick up the slack for coworkers or spread yourself thin. It just means developing the skill base to be competent regardless of the task. Like Inspector Gadget. If you're flexible and willing to take on new and unanticipated tasks, you'll become highly valued by everybody around you.

At the same time, you should also develop a specialty—something at which you're absolutely brilliant and for which you're the go-to guy or gal. Maybe you create the best

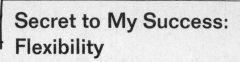

Secret to My Success: Flexibility

by Patrice, Nurse

Fresh out of college with a nursing degree, I was the new kid on the block on the Labor and Delivery floor at a large teaching hospital in Baltimore. All of the other nurses were much older and were way more experienced, so I struggled at first with finding ways to excel on the job.

Then I realized that every employee should have a gimmick—something positive that you're known for in the workplace. My gimmick was my schedule flexibility.

I was the only nurse on my floor without children, so when family emergencies came up for my colleagues, I would make my best effort to switch shifts with them. Not only was I flexible about the hours I worked, but I was also easygoing about working where I was needed, even if it meant going to another floor for that day.

By using these tactics, I gained both popularity with staff as well as experience in various divisions of the hospital. So I don't even need a gimmick anymore. I'm just an all-around expert.

PowerPoint presentations, or can always suggest new ways to approach something, or no one in the world knows more about marketing bleach than you do. Find your niche and let it be known.

If you can do a lot but do something amazingly well, you're golden!

Dog-Ear This Page

Peter is the director of program development for a nonprofit organization in Massachusetts, and he is a fountain of knowledge regarding the necessities for success in the workplace. Prepare to underline.

Convey Persistence and Loyalty

"Don't job hop in the early stages of your career. It can be interesting and fun to move from job to job, but staying with a job for more than a couple years can pay off in valuable experience and higher wages.

"In most organizations, the best work gets assigned to reliable, committed, and productive employees, and it takes at least a couple years to build your reputation."

Hone Management Skills

"Every organization needs people who understand basic management, and the best work and best pay are available to employees who can effectively organize people, money, and systems. Even if your career aim is not to work in management, learn those skills anyway and you'll have a better chance at getting the type of assignments that most interest you.

"Young people, and especially young women, often shy away from management opportunities, but in many cases the best managers are those who take on the role reluctantly."

Create Tangible Products

"Organizations struggle to measure productivity in employees. Many employees show up every day, have good attitudes, and toil long hours, but don't routinely bring their efforts to fruition. In approaching your work, think in terms of creating products, closing deals, resolving conflicts, writing reports, organizing resources, building systems, recruiting talented people, and other tangible outcomes.

"Make yourself useful to the organization by creating things that other people need and use, and then put yourself in charge of what you've created. Products can be small, like setting up the staff telephone list, or big, like writing a major proposal. Eventually, you'll be viewed by the organization as the expert, 'owner,' or manager of something important that you've created."

Stay Positive and Poised

"Many people spend most of their waking hours at work, and life is tough enough without having to deal with negative, combative, rude bozos at the office. Your attitude at work plays a huge role in professional success. Cultivate the best parts of your personality, show people consideration, and offer genuine encouragement to your colleagues.

"Even your boss will appreciate encouragement from you. Be a reliable, friendly coworker, but at the same time, show that you have poise, backbone, and integrity. But be careful— no one likes the wimpy, cheerleader type."

Performance Review

What better way to see what's coming than to see what's coming? Here's a sample performance review. Look closely at the behaviors that are assessed, the various points of measurement, and the different ways an employee can be evaluated.

Each company's human resources department will have its own performance review criteria available in written form. If you're not given a copy of these criteria when you're hired, ask for them.

Productivity

- Knows his or her job well
- Develops a good plan for completing projects
- Prioritizes tasks and effectively handles multiple responsibilities
- Develops thoughtful drafts and produces good work products
- Responds to changes and new approaches well
- Handles obstacles effectively
- Manages time and work effectively

Reliability

- Arrives on time
- Comes to meetings on time and participates as planned
- Accomplishes tasks according to agreed schedules
- Pays attention to detail and checks work for accuracy
- Can be relied upon to produce a complete product
- Notices things that need to be done and takes charge

Communication Skills
- Offers good ideas
- Writes clearly and uses correct grammar and punctuation
- Is a good listener
- Speaks clearly and confidently
- Gives clear instructions
- Effective advocate for company mission
- Discusses work needs with supervisor

Relationships
- Maintains good, cooperative relationships with coworkers
- Responds to the needs of others
- Contributes to team work
- Builds relationships with people of all backgrounds
- Works to gather diverse perspectives
- Expresses his or her perspective in an open, nonthreatening manner

Fiscal Management
- Uses cost-saving measures
- Effectively monitors project spending
- Efficiently follows budgetary processes and procedures
- Adheres to travel policies and procedures

Cooperation and Responsiveness
- Holds himself or herself accountable
- Demonstrates good judgment in deciding when to work independently or check in with supervisor

- Follows directions well

- Open to suggestions and constructive criticism

- Incorporates corrections or other feedback

Supervisory Abilities

- Is decisive

- Delegates authority effectively

- Provides direction and vision

- Motivates staff

- Adheres to personnel policies

- Promotes cooperation and teamwork

- Encourages and listens to suggestions

- Resolves complaints and issues

- Provides guidance and support as needed

- Balances need for staff autonomy and direction

- Is accessible to staff

- Shows interest in staff professional development

Sitting at the Grown-Up Table

All great success stories share a common ingredient: initiative. Whether you look at Thomas Edison, Martin Luther King, Jr., Michael Jordan, the woman in the corner office, or the salesman who started with nothing, all of them realized that their goals were only attainable if they demonstrated

Ben's Corner

I wanted to write more and I noticed that our PR department was struggling to fill their monthly newsletters. So I began helping them in my free time, which satisfied one of my professional goals, demonstrated initiative, and created allies for me in another department. Excelling involves identifying a company's need and actually doing something about it.

drive, enthusiasm, and *cojones*. They showed initiative even when it went unrecognized.

Oh, crap. We've just hit a cliché. *Success is a matter of taking initiative*. But that's okay, because there's always some value to these trite truisms that every parent knows.

When you first arrive at a new job, you're in a unique position to see its flaws in processes, structure, and protocol. You have fresh eyes. It's critical to maintain this outsider's viewpoint, as Bruno, an alumni coordinator in his late twenties, indicates:

Take initiative when you're working—use an "outside-in" approach. Find what the company needs and see whether you can, or feel interested in, filling that niche.

Rachel is a thirty-something managing director of a nonprofit, and she suggests:

Always tell your supervisor that you want more responsibilities. Otherwise he or she may think that you're satisfied with what you're doing. Being able to set clear boundaries, however, may be even more difficult to learn, but in the long run makes you more efficient and effective.

Head of the Class

Professional growth is critical. Often, people leave jobs when opportunities for development and learning decrease or disappear. Taking classes, at night or on the weekends, is a superb way to continue growing as a person and a professional. And frequently, companies will offer to pay for all or part of position-related coursework or programs.

Marcia, a layout and content specialist in PR, has significantly improved her talents, versatility, and value as an employee through numerous classes outside of work. Exploring courses in graphic design, writing, editing, and marketing, she continues to diversify her capabilities. She urges: "Adult education is tops, especially if you have a liberal arts degree and need solid work skills or experience, or if you need to alter your career path."

Look in the Mirror, Quick

After beginning a position at a new company, you'll typically have a performance review after about four to six months. This meeting, while for some terrifying, is good and necessary. Swear, we're not lying. Remember, your boss is not looking for a way to fire you but instead a means to evaluate how well you're accomplishing your tasks and handling your

Ben's Corner

I've come to realize that company funds to support staff development are finite. So find out when your firm's fiscal year begins. By making my requests early, I've significantly increased my chances of receiving reimbursement for a class or other work-related activity.

responsibilities. Performance reviews are your chance to shine. So brush your teeth, shower well, and prepare thoroughly.

Okay, here's the money shot: Evaluate yourself first. It can't be overstressed how essential frequent self-assessments are. Get into the habit of checking your own progress every few weeks.

- What projects have you participated in?
- How did you contribute to them?
- Were the efforts successful?
- In what concrete, measurable way did you assist with reaching the projects' goals?

Think of anecdotes or examples that represent each category best. Collect work samples. And take a Valium.

(Im) Balance

In an ideal world, many of us would find the perfect balance between work and our personal lives. But this ain't no ideal

Ben's Corner

I was completely caught off guard when a supervisor asked me to assess his performance as my boss during my performance evaluation. A twisted question, wasn't it? But I didn't want to squander the opportunity to improve a few work dynamics that weren't so great, so I used tact, I followed each critique with praise, and I chose my battles carefully.

world, now is it? What this means is that sacrifices are a reality of excelling professionally.

While companies are increasingly allowing more flexible schedules for employees, and while technologies that support remote employees are becoming more prevalent, in most cases, work will demand compromises outside of work.

Matt, a chemistry grad student at UC–Berkeley, explains:

If you want to be the best, you're going to have to be "imbalanced." For example, if you want to be a professor in a major research university, then you really have to put in tremendous amounts of time and sacrifice other things in your life that you enjoy doing, at least on a temporary basis.

As you surely know well, life consists of an endless series of choices. Whether you're a corporate executive or in an entry-level position, it's vital for you to tackle urgent tasks and set your priorities. But as much as we can wish for balance, the stone-cold truth is that getting ahead professionally often re-quires personal sacrifices.

Total Recall

- Actively and consciously market the brand "you" be-cause no one else will. Don't be afraid to sell yourself.

- Share your successes with your supervisor. Remember that actions speak louder than words—do your best, go beyond what's expected, and keep track of your accom-plishments.

- Do great work and make sure to actually create tangible products that illustrate that great work.

- Initiative: Take it. As much as possible.

- Be flexible and volunteer to take on a variety of tasks, but make sure to develop your own niche and let the world know about it.

- Capitalize on all opportunities for personal development. Focus on constant, neverending improvement. Because if you don't, the next guy or gal will.

- Prepare for your performance review. Consider the goals and objectives that you set with your supervisor when you began your position. Think about the questions that your supervisor will ask. Be ready and be confident.

7

Movin' on Up

(or requesting a promotion or a raise)

So, you've become a pro at this job stuff. You and your boss see eye to eye at least some of the time, your colleagues respect you, and you've been busy working on one grand project after another. Time to shift into lower gear and cruise through your workdays.

Not. It's time to think about your future at the company and consider asking for a promotion or a raise. And when's the right time to ask about a promotion? Well, it's not the right time after you've gotten poor feedback in your current position. Or if you haven't mastered the responsibilities you already have. It's also not the right time if your company is in a financial or some other kind of crisis.

The good news is that there *are* lots of right times, too. You've been earning excellent reviews. You've been given more duties lately by your supervisors. Someone in your company with the position you want just left. You get the point.

Chances are that if you've been getting good vibes, then you're not wrong. Read on to see how to make your move.

- Success Scrapbook
- Finding Allies
- 007
- Make a Date
- Okay, So It's Not Doubling Your Salary
- Take It or Leave It

Success Scrapbook

Before you ask for a raise or a promotion, you need to lay your trap. Quietly yet effectively begin to build both a tangible and an invisible portfolio to present when it's time to go in for the kill.

Remember the way mom used to save all the programs from your dance recitals and sporting events? Use her as a model. As you go about your duties at your job, keep copies of your outstanding work. Leah, a thirty-something assistant buyer in Boston, says,

> I always save reports that I'm asked to write, and if I'm sending an important letter or email out, I'll sometimes "cc:" it to my boss. That way they know that I'm getting things done on my end.

But beware: There is such a thing as too much. Consider what you share, when, and with whom.

You should also keep a record of activities that you organized and new systems or processes that you implemented. The more concrete and permanent, the better. Especially make note if these positive contributions to the office were outside the realm of your assigned tasks.

Sharifa, a government student in Cambridge, remembers:

> When I was at a summer internship a few years ago, their records were very disorganized. One day I didn't have a lot to do, so I started refiling everything. I would work on that whenever my work slowed down. They were so happy—I could do no wrong for the rest of my time there.

When your employer is considering whether to give you more responsibilities, anecdotes like this one will be critical.

Sure, in theory, your supervisor should know about your achievements and progress—and some of you might luck out with an attentive and caring boss like that. But in most cases you have to be your own cheerleader and promoter to get the kudos and advancement you deserve. This might feel strange at first, but you've got to find ways to do it that you're comfortable with. Otherwise, you might end up waiting forever for someone to notice how awesome you are and give you more responsibility and more money.

Finding Allies

In addition to keeping track of your achievements, you've got to make an "invisible" case for yourself. Employers tend to do some spying when making decisions about your future at the company. Since they can't watch you all the time, they rely on the opinions of others to influence their impressions of you. It's kind of like those flying monkeys who worked for the Wicked Witch in *The Wizard of Oz*—your boss has many eyes and ears. But this is not a bad thing. Each assignment, each colleague, and each meeting is an opportunity to impress and excel.

Engaging in the smooching of butt is not the way to create good references. The first way to make friends in the workplace is to simply do your job. Dayle, a medical student from Long Island, says,

> When someone doesn't carry his weight, other people have to pick up the slack. So the best way to stay on good terms with me is to make sure not to stick me with your work.

Be willing to do favors for people. Switch shifts with coworkers when convenient. Run an errand if it's on your way. Include someone on a project who would appreciate the exposure. And don't limit your favors to the higher-ups. Treat everyone at your job with respect.

Jon, a newly hired elementary school teacher in Pennsylvania, recalls a piece of advice he received when he started his job:

> An older teacher told me that the two people who deserve the most respect from you at work are the custodian and the secretary. You'll probably need them more than anyone else.

Oftentimes, senior workers will ask people under you for their opinion of your performance. Remember that the spies are often well disguised.

Rachel's Corner

Several times, I've had promotions offered to me when I'd never even inquired about them. I've since asked, what makes someone look like the right candidate for a job that they don't even seem to want? Above all, employers want workers who go above and beyond their job description. People in high places also take notice of everyday skills that could be useful in a leadership position: an obsession with organization, practical thinking, and the ability to give clear instructions. I've discovered that sometimes one can be applying for a promotion and not even know it. The process can be long term and you may not get much verbal information, but don't sleep—big brother is watching.

007

Since you're surrounded by spies, why not become one yourself? It's time to do some investigating. You can't just go and ask for a promotion without a specific idea as to what is available in the organization. Become well informed about the goings-on of human resources and about promotion politics.

Talk to coworkers about their experience in the company. How long do people usually work there before getting a promotion? Some companies have very clear standards and time horizons for promoting workers, while others are more flexible. Has there been any talk of people leaving positions? What's the protocol for alerting supervisors that one desires a position change?

We Talk With . . .

Kate, Health Policy Analyst

How should one prepare for seeking a promotion or a raise?
Make sure that you keep track of your accomplishments, large
and small, throughout your tenure in a certain job position.

*Doesn't that sometimes come off as if you're bragging about a
job well done?*
It doesn't always come naturally to feel as if you're tooting your
own horn. However, it's so important to keep a record of your
achievements, both for yourself as well as in a more formal
way, to share it with your supervisor and your colleagues. By
doing this, you'll ensure that they know the valuable work that
you're doing, and it helps a great deal in your advancing within
the company.

*What are some practical ways to keep the higher-ups aware
of your accomplishments?*
I never would've done this even a couple years ago because it
seemed too self-serving, but now, if I have a meeting or a project that I feel goes very well, I'll email the vice president of our
department to share details about it. Then I'm not waiting until
my review to recount my met goals and various successes.

You might be surprised at how easy it is to obtain information. All it takes is money, because everyone's got a price.
Okay, bad idea. Instead, go the legal route and talk to coworkers and your friends in HR. Also visit the website of your company to get a feel of what the hiring climate is at the moment.

A quick visit to www.monster.com will reveal how extensively your company is currently searching and for which positions.

Make a Date

You've done all of the setup, so it's time to go for it. Take a deep breath and try not to be too anxious. Dawud, a graphic designer who graduated from college in 1998, encourages:

> Asking for a raise or a promotion shouldn't be that hard. After all, you already work there, which means that they liked you the first time you interviewed with them. This is just the natural follow-up.

Make an appointment to talk to your supervisor—don't just catch him when he happens to "look free." You want to make sure he has time to speak to you in depth. Also, scheduling a time in advance shows your seriousness about the issue.

When you begin speaking, it's important to strike a balance: Be assertive, but not demanding. Try beginning with a joke involving a rabbi, a priest, and a nun. Well, maybe not, but you get the point.

You should start off with a few sentences stating your feelings about your experience at the job so far. Joanne, a public health student, suggests:

> Tell your boss that you've felt supported in your position and that you've enjoyed the work. Give a few examples of things that you've learned from the job.

The hardest part will be when you say you want a change. Stating that you're ready for new challenges is one way to term the request. Another approach is to say that you were wondering about opportunities for growth within the company. If you're asking for a raise, you're going to have to come out and say that in some way. It's not easy, we know, but borrow from Nike and Just Do It!

After you state your purpose for calling the meeting, it's time to win over your boss with your compelling argument. Review your successes from your scrapbook and talk about things you'd like to work on and new responsibilities you'd like to take on. As you do, make sure to emphasize why you think you can do those things extremely well.

Don't put your employer on the spot by forcing an answer right then and indicate that you're open to further discussion. Don't make any threats, either. The "promote me or I'm outta here" method is a bit too *Jerry Maguire*. Instead of showing you the money, they might show you the door.

Okay, So It's Not Doubling Your Salary

If you go into that meeting and get everything you want, congratulations. You da (wo)man. But most likely, you'll leave with a partial victory. Perhaps the raise isn't what you'd hoped. Maybe the promotion is in name only, and your responsibilities will be largely the same. Or the position change might not be available for another six weeks. Whatever it is, don't be discouraged.

I Foresaw It
by Fannie, Investment Reporting
Consultant

When negotiating an offer for a position, a raise, or a promotion, keep in mind a great mnemonic that I learned in grad
school. The acronym is I FORESAW IT:

Interest Mine, hers (my boss's), ours. Beyond the respective
demands, why do we each want what we say we want? Rank
the answers in order of importance. Include intangible interests
such as face saving. Don't skimp on common interests (that is,
shared goals you can achieve by working together).

Factual Research Knowledge counts. What do industry experts say? What published information is there about the
salaries in your field? How is the organization set up? Who is the
ultimate decision maker? Err on the side of exhaustive learning.

Options Brainstorm possible deal terms. That is, think of as
many negotiable solutions to the problem as possible, even if
they seem silly. Salary, bonus, vacation days, sick days, tuition
reimbursement, professional memberships, accelerated performance review, gym passes, etc. Get help from friends or colleagues on this. Review and refine your options and select the
ones you feel would be your first preference.

Reactions and Responses Do this last. Once you develop offers using the rest of the mnemonic, practice proposing your
offer to your boss and try predicting her reactions to your proposal and to the situation generally. What will she feel she'll lose
if she says yes and gain if she says no? Anticipate and consider
how you might respond. Consider her interests. How will she sat-
isfy her interests by saying yes and hurt them by saying no? Are
there independent criteria you can use to show the proposal is
fair? Role playing can produce real surprises and insights.

Empathy and Ethic Empathize. Put yourself in the other person's shoes. Speak or write a paragraph in his or her voice about the situation. What problem does he or she have? Why do you seem difficult? What hangups are you bringing to the negotiation? How would you like to be treated if you were in her place?

Setting and Scheduling Where will you meet? Where are you each more comfortable? Will you meet via phone? Email? (Phone negotiations tend to fail more than face-to-face negotiations do. Emails tend to fail even more.) When will you meet? Timing is crucial. What time of day will you meet? Avoid doing so when you're tired and the other person is busy.

Alternatives to Agreement If there's no deal, what will you do instead? What will she do? List the different possible alternatives separately for each side. Try to improve your alternatives with research. Rank yours—which is your best alternative? Your worst? Rank hers. Which is her best? Her worst? (If she says no to your terms, she may be running the risk of winding up with her worst alternatives. Tactfully noting this risk may encourage her to say yes). Alternatives matter.

Who Who can influence the outcome of the talks? Consider the various parties you interviewed with and levels above. Who will you deal with? HR? Is there someone else who would be better to deal with instead? Managers tend to have much more latitude than HR.

Independent Criteria What objective standards can you appeal to so the other person feels your offer is fair and reasonable? Look for something the other person is likely to trust that's out of your control: MBA graduate average, industry salary survey, verifiable precedent, existing contracts, etc. Independent criteria let you say, in effect, "Don't take my word for it; let's turn to something we both trust." That's far more persuasive than saying, "Well, I think I'm making you a very fair offer."

Topics, Targets, and Trade-Offs The crux of the entire preparation. This is where you turn all the preparation work into a focused, one-page guide to the talk. In essence, you set an agenda, develop goals for each, prioritize, and add some promising creative options. Keep this with you during your meeting to help you stay focused and on track.

The I FORESAW IT mnemonic serves as a checklist, reminding you of many of the factors to think about. Use it and you'll feel more confident going into your promotion or compensation negotiation. You'll also be more willing to listen to the counterarguments because you have less reason to feel threatened—you've done your homework.

Todd, a twenty-seven-year-old market researcher in New York, says:

If you're fairly new on the job and they agree to give you anything, big or small, be grateful. The market is always competitive, so they must value you if they're giving you more than you had.

Take It or Leave It

Worst-case scenario: You get denied. Your disappointment may deepen based on how long you've been with the organization, how much you like your current position, and how desperate you are for more cash.

As you cope with these issues, you have to ask yourself the difficult question of whether you want to stay, even without

Beauty and the Beast

by Eugenia, Former Communications Coordinator

I used to work as a communications coordinator for a beauty company in New York, but I had problems with my supervisor from the start. I tried to work things out but the situation kept getting worse, until I couldn't work for her any longer.

I really liked the company, however, and wanted to stay on board, so I broached the subject of changing departments after one year of working under my supervisor. One year is a long time in an unhappy work situation, but I wanted to show the company that I was committed to trying to work things out.

Throughout that year, I recorded the problems I had with my supervisor and periodically went to Human Resources to give them updates on the situation.

Meanwhile, I focused on my work and tried very hard to do a good job. I wanted to show them that I could work well under pressure and that the issues I had with my boss hadn't affected my ability to fulfill my duties.

The company made every effort to find me a position in an-other subdivision, putting out feelers in the offices of the other departments. While they did find me an equal-paying position elsewhere, the job description didn't match what I was looking for. In the end I decided to leave the company, but with no ill feeling. I feel like they did their best to try to work with me.

the raise, promotion, or position change. If you decide that it's time to pack your bags, Mike, an engineering graduate student, says:

> Explain to your employer that you enjoyed your time there, but you have needs that can no longer be met. Don't make it personal. It's possible that your boss wanted to help you out, but it just couldn't happen.

Whatever you decide, don't burn bridges by being angry and antagonistic toward your boss. The more professional you act, the greater your chances of succeeding the next time—or getting a good reference if you decide to leave.

Total Recall

- Don't be too timid, intimidated, or shy to ask for a raise or a promotion when you think you deserve it. Your success is your responsibility.

- Create a success scrapbook to record your accomplishments on the job. The more evidence, the better.

- Establish references or allies in the company who can vouch for you and your work. Supervisors frequently ask colleagues for input on your performance. Anticipate this.

- If you're interested in a position change, keep a vigilant eye on which positions are currently available at your company. Stay well-informed of HR activity to capitalize on staffing changes or openings. Is your company presently posting any openings on different job sites?

- Schedule an appointment with your supervisor to talk about your promotion or raise, as opposed to just dropping by. This type of a conversation should not be impromptu but planned and arranged beforehand.

- During a meeting with your supervisor or boss, maintain realistic expectations and be willing to compromise. Make your case, be confident, and don't expect an answer right away.

- Consider the pros and cons of leaving if you're not granted your position change request. Whatever you do, be professional.

8

I Got Next

(or finding your next gig)

At one point or another in your career, you'll decide to change jobs. From our experience, this is something you'll do quite a bit early on as you search for your true calling—or maybe just a bigger paycheck. Change is often good, but make sure that you're making it at the right time and for the right reasons. We offer some suggestions on how to figure out when it might be right, so keep reading.

The truth is that finding that next job can be hard work. Unless you're a Bush, a Kennedy, or a Forbes, the road to a great job—and even an okay job—will be paved with your own sweat. So grab a Gatorade—it's game time.

- Set Roots
- The Six-Month Itch: Leaving So Soon?

- Take the Leap
- Before You Bounce
- Challenge Yourself, Daniel-Son
- Expect Some Bumps in the Road

Set Roots

For three important reasons, you shouldn't consider the next job until you've set firm roots in your current job.

First, your job and your boss deserve some dedication. Jay, that former career counselor from chapter 1, stresses this point:

There's training involved in a job, and people don't hire new employees for them to leave right away. Nobody expects someone to leave after six months. In most organizations, employers want employees to stay for a couple of years.

Second, it's common to be fooled in one way or another in the first months on a job. Perhaps you only start out doing menial tasks, but then the job and your responsibilities grow more gratifying and challenging. And among those seemingly annoying colleagues you might find a few who're wonderful, friendly, and great to work with.

Third, you have to consider your résumé and the message it conveys to potential employers. How will you look if you don't stay at companies longer than six months? Why would a future employer ever consider hiring a chronic job-hopper?

The Six-Month Itch: Leaving So Soon?

While there are reasons to stick it out at your job for a while, you owe it to yourself to evaluate your job from time to time and make sure that you're working there for good reasons. Once you've learned the ropes of your job and had your share of office drama, it's time to ask yourself some questions:

- Are you excited when a new week of work begins?
- How often are you checking the clock during the day?
- Do your assignments challenge and engage you?
- If the pros of changing jobs appear equal to those of staying put, what do your gut feelings tell you?

But even if your answers to these questions are: "No, every ten minutes, no, and *leave*," take a breath and pause to hear the following bits of wise advice before you take off for your next gig.

Alexia, a law student, shares this insight:

Six months into my first job, I knew that I didn't want to remain there for long, so I used it as a learning experience. What I learned is that marketing yourself doesn't end once you've been hired. Remember that it's a process just like anything else. All you can do is set realistic goals and aim for progress, not perfection.

Terry, a director of state policy development for a non-profit, seconds this advice about progressing toward your ideal position:

Treat every job with importance and give it your best. It may not be the job you're dreaming of, but it may teach you enough to realize your dream position.

And Jenn, a recent graduate and analyst for a consulting firm, gives this tip:

Expect to settle into your first postcollegiate position but realize that it may not be your career. Get the most out of the experience, learn from it, and when you're ready, move on.

Bottom line: Don't rush to judgment, give every job a fair shot, and be brutally honest about your reasons for wanting to leave. This will help you avoid making a mistake and increase the chances that your next job is closer to what you're after.

Take the Leap

Remaining in even the most run-of-the-mill position can feel pretty seductive when compared to the unknown of that next job. You can't help but wonder if you're giving up a good thing. Like other aspects of life, change can provoke great anxiety— even if you absolutely, positively know that you want to leave, having qualms about changing jobs is completely normal.

Don't feel rushed to choose your next job because feeling rushed blows, and especially as you select your position. Matt, Chemistry Boy, believes that when you make the decision to look for the next job, it should be informed by knowledge and careful consideration:

Hotlanta: Not So Hot
by Anita, Teacher

In a rush to leave Boston, I accepted the first teaching position offered to me at an elementary school in Atlanta. While the first few months involved adjusting to a new set of rules and procedures, as well as learning a new language (the southern version of English), I felt more or less comfortable in my position.

As the year progressed, however, I began to feel as if the position that I chose was not ideal. The administrative staff wasn't supportive of my needs as a new teacher. Also, as I spoke to other teachers in nearby school systems, I realized that there were many better teaching positions for which I was qualified.

Recently, I've been visiting other schools as I search for a new job. To prevent myself from settling when choosing a new school, I've prioritized what I need in a school and made a list of questions to ask during interviews.

I've realized that I need an environment that has a school-wide discipline system with consequences, as well as ample technology and parental involvement. Being new to the city, I will also look for a younger staff because it's been hard to make friends in a school of veteran teachers.

Loving my job would've made a difference in my comfort level here in Atlanta. I can't guarantee that I'll find the perfect work environment for the next school year, but I can be sure to allow myself options and maintain clear expectations.

My advice is to make sure you do your research and give yourself enough time to do the research so that you really understand your options, don't feel rushed, and can make a good decision based on good understanding of what's available.

Ari's Corner

I had serious doubts when I left my job teaching Spanish at a private high school to become a bilingual teacher at a public elementary school. I feared I was trading comfort and freedom for longer hours, more bureaucracy, and the grueling task of teaching reading, writing, and math (for the first time), and in my second language to boot. Taking risks had always paid off before, but I was nervous that I'd regret taking the leap. Looking back on the decision, this new job was exactly what I needed.

If you've decided that it's time for a change, remember to treat your current employer with respect. It would be ridiculously unfair to give two-days notice to a boss. Aim for two- to four-weeks notice, depending on your role at the company and the difficulty they'll have in replacing you.

When telling your boss about your decision to leave, don't get personal. Explain your reasons, be polite, and expect that he or she might be surprised by your decision and get upset. For extra points, ask how you can help better manage your transition. Even on your way out, it pays to leave a good impression.

Mike, a recent grad and salesperson for an Internet company, shares:

No matter how much you resent a past employer, never burn your bridges. You never know when your paths will cross again or when you'll need a good reference.

Don't Let Your Fear of Change Stop You

by Shane, Teacher

There's a step that comes before finding a new job. Many people forget this step. First, you must leave your old job. This is much easier said than done.

I gave the Teach for America program a two-year commitment. They placed me in the poorest school district in our country: Sunflower, Mississippi. By the end of the first year, I knew this wasn't the job for me, but I didn't quit. Why?

1. I'd made a commitment.

2. I didn't want to admit that I failed.

3. I forgot that an infinite number of alternatives existed outside the confines of that county.

Be careful about making commitments. Don't be afraid to break them if they're coming at the expense of your sanity, pocketbook, or potential. Admit failure. Know that the grass often *is* greener on the other side.

Six years later, I'm still teaching. I enjoy it more and I've gotten quite good at it. Nonetheless, teaching lacks three things that are becoming more important to me as I near my thirties: money, respect, and leadership.

Don't let your fear of change stop you from switching gears or starting over. Find a job that excites you. Teaching doesn't excite me much anymore. I like writing stories, following my stock portfolio, and helping people solve their problems. Looks like it's time for another career change.

Before You Bounce

Jay, our resident career expert, provides us with a few valuable ideas for what to do before changing jobs.

Before Jumping Ship, Navigate the Waters

"If you're feeling restless, you honestly owe it to yourself to be looking. Get on your computer for an hour in the evening and check out any available opportunities. Keep your sights broad. Keep exploring and don't stop exploring because you have a job. Unless you can afford a few weeks without a paycheck, it's usually wise to keep the steady salary of your current job as you search for the next one."

Watch, Listen, and Learn

"Assuming you've been there long enough to not feel like you're skipping out, then my advice is to really learn about the other jobs. As you connect with people through your work, learn about what they do. This can help guide your future job choices."

Sew Up Support

"Here's the other thing you should always do at any job: Have one or two strong supporters in the organization who will act as references for you in the future."

Challenge Yourself, Daniel-Son

If you're determined to find your next job, where do you start? Nabulungi, executive assistant extraordinaire, advises you to think big:

> Think of this as a brand new chapter in your life. Don't simply look for a "replacement" job, or something identical to what you were doing—don't settle for what's easy. Use this opportunity to challenge yourself and learn a new skill or life lesson.
>
> Also, don't necessarily go for what you are "good at," if it means avoiding something more challenging that you might enjoy. Ideally, your career should always stimulate, and doing something that comes easily may not necessarily fit this goal.

Think carefully about what you dislike about your current job and, even if you hate doing this, write those reasons down.

Ari's Corner

I received job offers from two different elementary schools. The first was highly respected, in an attractive neighborhood, and near my house. The second required a longer commute, was in a poor neighborhood, and despite talented teachers, was under attack for declining test scores. Some might say the decision was a no-brainer. But challenges always inspire me, so after hours of deliberation I picked the second school.

Tips for Changing Jobs

Job Searching while on the Job

- Job search before and after business hours, not during the day. You might get caught, and the repercussions can be unpleasant.

- Arrange interviews during your lunch hour if the company is nearby, or use a sick or personal day in other cases.

- Don't discuss your search with coworkers. It puts your colleagues in an awkward position and it makes you vulnerable to information leaks.

Get the Most from Your Current Employer

- Seek professional learning and experience from your employer before splitting for another. The point is to advance, not to plateau.

- A job represents references. Strengthen your relationships with individuals or supervisors who will be your references later.

- A job also represents a network. As you move through your career, networking becomes more effective as you build relationships with more people. Remember that your current colleagues can potentially help you snag jobs in the future.

How Not to Burn Bridges

- Give ample advance notice of a job change. Aim for one month's notice so that your employer has time to hire someone before you split.

- Offer to help hire, train, and orient your replacement. Knowledge transfer is crucial within companies, and the more that you can facilitate a smooth and seamless transition between yourself and your successor, the better.

- If you feel comfortable, check in with your former employer occasionaliy after you've left the company. For reasons of networking and job references, it just makes too much sense to keep in touch with former supervisors.

Keep these reasons close as you look for your next gig to make sure that you're looking for the right job characteristics that are likely to make you happy.

Expect Some Bumps in the Road

As you undoubtedly know by now, every job search has its low points: there aren't enough job listings in the area you're interested in, you don't seem to be having much luck with interviews, the cool jobs don't cover half of your monthly bills, and so on. It sucks, but it's part of the process.

The truth is that there are probably many jobs out there that will bring you career success and satisfaction. It may take a long time, a few wrong choices, and some difficult challenges, but you'll find your place. Have hope.

Chris, a twenty-nine-year-old freelance journalist in Boston, conveys some candid advice about the potential disappointments along the Yellow Brick Road on the way to your dream job.

Here it is: You're going to fail. I don't mean that in some all-encompassing, existential way. I have no doubt that you're smarter than the average Joe, that you excelled in school, and

We Talk With . . .

Mark, Independent Project Coordinator

What's it like having a nontraditional job? What are the advantages and disadvantages of always being your own boss?
The advantages are that you don't have someone ticking you off all the time by telling you what to do. And particularly if you have authority issues like I do, it spares you the problem of being "pushed around" by your boss. Conversely, it deprives you of guidance, wisdom, and support from an elder or mentor.

You don't have to show up at nine and stay until five—you set your own clock. The disadvantage is no one ever gives you time off—you have to give it to yourself, and sometimes that's hard.

Another advantage is you can really follow your instincts and intuitions about what the next step in your career should be. In other words, you don't have to be tied to an institution's agenda. But the disadvantage is that your work is not being leveraged by a large group working for a common purpose—it's you working on your own, trying to do it all by yourself, which can be daunting.

The upside is you can take the assignments you want and not the ones you don't, but as soon as one project ends, you're "unemployed" again.

What advice would you give to someone considering a more independent career path?
I'd recommend that you do both early in your career: Let yourself experience the nine-to-five approach and also the independent contractor approach. See how they feel—try them on. By the time you're thirty, make sure you've done some of both, set your course based on how it felt, and remember that neither way easily or necessarily leads to the promised land. They are two different paths, both filled with rewards and challenges.

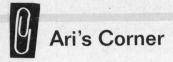

Ari's Corner

When I took that "next job" teaching elementary school, I had no idea if it would be a good fit. But it was enough for me to know that I'd grow from the challenge and that it would reveal whether teaching was the career for me. Thus far, my job has exceeded my hopes—it has everything I'd sought: meaningful interaction, the opportunity to inspire and nurture young people, and constant challenges and learning.

now the world is your oyster. You have big dreams, and you have what it takes to make them happen. But it's just as true that, somewhere along the line, you're going to come up short, or seemingly come up short.

Failure happens to most of us, and those who are ultimately successful understand that and don't let it defeat them utterly. The temptation is to believe that successful people are always successful and that when you fail, you fail alone. In fact, just the opposite is true.

The road to job success has its dips and potholes, but if you can be resilient, and if you can grow from both missteps and triumphs, you'll find your way. Honest.

Dave, an assistant principal, reminds us that persistence and perspective are crucial:

With your career, it's not a sprint but a marathon. You don't have to know everything right away and you don't have to do everything right away. There are going to be low times, and you have to pace yourself. It's all part of a process, so you have to keep your eyes on the prize and keep going.

Will adds:

You have to keep the faith, even in a down market. My patience comes from knowing that I *will* find something in the future. I'm young, no wife and kids—no other responsibilities—I can take risks. Hopefully, these risks will turn into great rewards.

Total Recall

- Make sure you've given a job some time before leaving. Every position has its honeymoon period, after which it rarely seems as perfect, special, or rewarding. Make sure that this isn't just another phase or that there isn't something you can do to make it better (see chapter 7).

- Understand the reasons for wanting to leave your job and keep them in mind as you search for your next one.

- Thoroughly research your next position or professional move before making any rash or drastic decisions. Take your time.

- Don't seek out an identical job to your current one. Instead, challenge yourself with something new in order to grow, explore, and learn professionally.

- When you leave, treat your boss and your colleagues with respect. Don't burn bridges—good relationships turn into a great network and strong references.

- Expect some bumps in the road toward job satisfaction and success, and learn from them. And always have hope—for every job that sucks, there's one you really enjoy. It might just take some time to find it.

9

Pinkslip.com

(or what to do after being laid off, fired, or having quit)

Ah, the beauties of the Internet. Dot-com, dot-org, dot-gov, dot-love . . . can you imagine life without email, Google, Amazon, and eBay? While we must tip our hats to the dot-com boom for its introduction of new avenues for communication and information, we can't forget its other popular legacy: layoffs.

Okay, fine, you're right: People were being laid off way before Pets.com retired its infamous sock puppet mascot. But in the past several years, the professional expectations and standards fundamental to many industries have shifted like never before. Due to the dot-com era and general economic landscape, résumés may now show a more varied background or shorter tenures in previous positions. And that's okay. Just be prepared to explain "what you learned" in those six weeks working for www.booger.com.

Bottom line—whether you're laid off or fired, or whether you willingly quit a position altogether, there could be a time in your twenties (or even thirties) when you're, well, y'know, "between jobs."

Understanding the opportunities that unemployment can present and the possibilities that await you can make this period in your life less scary and difficult. Time away from work allows you to focus on finding a better job, sleeping, internships, strengthening professional skills, self-assessments, sleeping, taking classes, and sleeping.

- Analyze This
- Get Up and Go to Work—Looking for a Job
- Developing Your Repertoire, Portfolio, and Other Big Words
- Take Risks
- School Is, Um, Cool
- Get the Bleep Outta Dodge

Analyze This

Denise is that director of human resources who rocked chapter 5. As you know, she personally hires, fires, and lays people off. Her principal advice concerns an in-depth self-evaluation following the cessation of work. (Ah, cessation, doesn't that sound better already?)

Ben's Corner

I've been laid off five times. Okay, you can stop laughing now. But it's true. The unexpected outcome of these layoffs, though, is that with each one I developed a clearer picture of what I wanted to do. Remember that those times between positions, whether intended or not, are ideal moments for reflection and self-evaluation.

If you've been laid off, generally the decision isn't made based on your performance but rather on a more objective need for the company to trim staff in order to reduce expenses. Depending upon how long you've been with the organization, I suggest getting right back out there to look. You want to find ways to affirm your worth. Other organizations asking you in to interview will be a confidence booster.

If you've been fired, understand what went wrong. This is difficult to do, especially if you strongly disagree with the decision. If lack of skills or knowledge was the reason, then that's something that can be gained over time (perhaps the job was simply not a good fit). If the reason was due to poor work habits, then a reality check might be in order. Try to look at the situation from the employer's perspective—that's hard to do, but it can be valuable.

It's not fun to think about why you're suddenly out of a job, but try. You'll thank yourself later.

Awkward but Important Details

When you leave a job, a number of new logistical issues arise. Here's a quick overview of some important matters:

Severance Pay

There are few laws regarding how much a company is obligated to pay you if it's laying you off. Your payout could be as little as nothing or as much as six months of salary. Thank you, United States government, for looking out for the little man.

Accrued Vacation Payout

Usually, your company must pay you the full value of any vacation time that you've accrued but haven't used. You usually receive this whether you've been laid off, fired, or have left on your own free will.

Collecting Unemployment

The amount that you're entitled to collect depends on the state in which you work. Which means it's time to hit Google. Each state has a Department of Labor website that explains everything you need to know about filing for unemployment. Your friends in HR should also be able to help with this.

COBRA Health Insurance

You can continue your health insurance after leaving a company thanks to the COBRA Act of 1986. Under COBRA, you pay 100 percent of your health insurance premium but at the discounted group rate that your company receives. Without COBRA, you pay a lot more.

401(k) or 403(b) Funds

Leaving a company doesn't mean losing your funds—once in your account, they're yours. Talk to HR and find out the details for rolling over your balance. You can combine it with your new account at your new job or have it managed by a completely independent investment firm.

Get Up and Go to Work— Looking for a Job

Finding yourself unemployed and searching for a job again can almost be nostalgic. (Just think, it brings us all the way back to chapter 1.) And it can also be frustrating or even depressing. So remember three points. First, the layoff wasn't your fault. Second, they won't ever know about those office supplies you "borrowed." Third, your previous position and experience will help and simplify a new job search.

Sara has boatloads of advice regarding the job search. She should know—she used to teach this very subject to inmates (no joke). So sit up straight, pop some Ritalin, and focus.

Step One: Get Out of Bed

"Make sure you schedule your weekdays like a work day. Get up by 7:00 am, shower, and get dressed. Check websites where your resume is posted, make follow-up calls, and research jobs that you're interested in to find out what skills and experience are necessary."

Ben's Corner

There's nothing more important than structuring your days of unemployment. Sleep and TV are omniscient, ubiquitous demons, and they will find you. I swear it. If you're not exceptionally disciplined, consider job hunting outside your apartment, whether in a library, at a friend's place, or in a café. I'm willing to share something embarrassing to make a point. It was when I was unemployed and without structured days that I started watching *Oprah*. Yes, you read that correctly: *Oprah*. Enough said.

Step Two: Turn Off the TV

"Take a lunch break, and use this hour for personal communication and down time. Then, get back to work on your job search. Don't get into the habit of running errands during normal work hours and don't 'reward' an hour's hard work job hunting with two hours of TV time (or other nonproductive activities). Job hunting is a job and should be treated like one. Follow a routine."

Step Three: Write Stuff Down

"Keep track of all jobs for which you apply. No employer wants to receive numerous résumes from one person for the same position—it makes you appear unorganized. Keep a printed copy of each job description in case an employer is interested in your résume and calls."

We Talk With . . .

Neil, Researcher

What can be gained from having been laid off, fired, or having quit a job?

It's an opportunity to start over, maybe change directions if you weren't happy with your old direction. It's also an opportunity to test your mettle. The task of finding a new job is a tough challenge. There's a great deal to be learned in the process.

What are common mistakes after having been laid off, fired, or having quit a job?

The most common mistake is to think that it's a convenient time for a vacation and then to take off for a month and spend money in the process. A second mistake is to think that getting back on a payroll will be an easy matter. A third mistake is to take things as they come without taking stock, marshalling your resources, and making things happen the way you want them to.

If you were suddenly laid off, fired, or quit your job, what would you do? How would you respond?

Take a few days, a week at the most, to figure out what happened and what your options are and to formulate a plan. Finding a new job is hard work and will require fortitude and drive. It's a full-time job: forty hours a week, five days a week, nine to five, minimum. Understand that it can take six months to a year to get the job you want. Get properly psyched for it. Learn how to interview, find some buddies to share war stories with, and remember that ten no's a week for twenty-five weeks followed by one yes means you have a job. Don't allow yourself to get discouraged.

Developing Your Repertoire, Portfolio, and Other Big Words

Jules was unemployed for more than a year, so she knows what's up. If there were ever a credential for this chapter, she's got it. We'll let her explain the rest.

Developing Yourself

"When I was unemployed, I did some volunteer work. I traveled. I was always writing and reading. All of these things were vital to maintaining my skills (and sanity), keeping me engaged in the world around me, and preventing me from driving my friends crazy."

Developing Your Network

"I did informational interviews—I called anyone who had a job I was interested in and who I thought would be generous enough to talk to me for half an hour. I investigated tons of different careers this way and I learned how people got their jobs. Doing informational interviews allowed me to think more broadly about what people do (besides become doctors, lawyers, and writers) and allowed me to make great networking connections."

Developing Your Skills

"If I had this time again I would've interned in a company that I was interested in but didn't have the skills or experience to get myself a real job there. I always thought I might get a job in the next few days or weeks, and that kept me from learning a new business. People hardly ever say no to free help, and I think that any experience is good experience, even if only for a few days or weeks. So my advice: Consider interning for a while if you can't find a full-time job."

Take Risks

When we're working nine to five every day, it's hard to find time to continue building our professional skill set. Far too often, jobs consist of a small handful of repetitive tasks. But what about your desire to master Adobe Photoshop, or that curiosity about marketing? Or that plan to backpack through China, or that aspiration to finally understand the mysteries of accounting and finance?

Time off is perfect for trying new things and taking risks. We'll spare you the fortune cookie clichés, but you know what people say about taking risks: Take them. Risk taking is an exceptional way to learn new things about yourself, to increase your versatility, and to expand your professional portfolio. So take a deep breath and jump.

Rachel is currently the managing director of a nonprofit. But she has boldly explored numerous jobs in the past, from TV and film production to entertainment public relations to job counseling to random temping assignments. She explains:

During a year when I was "between jobs," I took on many part-time jobs that paid the bills, gave me a very wide range of

Ben's Corner

Just out of college, I wanted more writing and editorial experience. But since I didn't have any, no one was willing to give me any (ouch, my brain hurts). Which is why I helped a woman edit and compile a collection of Jewish lesbian erotica. Now I've got your attention. I gained three things. First, work experience. Second, some incredible stories to share with friends. Third, some incredible stories to share with friends (well, there were so many).

experiences that fulfilled some work fantasies, and broadened my repertoire of skills to bring to the workplace.

School Is, Um, Cool

Another avenue for growth during time off is classes. There are endless opportunities out there, endless subjects to explore. Pauline feels strongly about this point:

This is a no-brainer. Take a class. I honestly can't think of anything else that would be more productive until the next opportunity for work comes along. Just make sure that it's a class that will enhance your growth potential in your field.

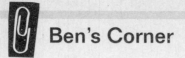

Ben's Corner

No matter what your industry or intended path, witnessing how other people live will teach you more than most college classes. I regard my six months in Ecuador as essential to who I am because I observed lifestyles diametrically opposed to my own. I also swam with giant tortoises in the Galapagos Islands, climbed the highest active volcano in the world, and fished for piranhas in the Amazon jungle. Don't forget that significant learning can happen outside the classroom and outside the office building.

Get the Bleep Outta Dodge

Dan is a database administrator in his late twenties who left America when he graduated from college. He sees this decision as a critical step in his development as a person and as a professional.

Dan recounts:

> As far as traveling, I definitely recommend taking some significant time off for everyone after college. It must sound clichéd, but I came back knowing myself much better than before, and my priorities in life became much clearer during that experience.

If you can afford it, consider traveling or working abroad at some point after college or after being laid off from a job. It may help you gain perspective on what career path to follow

A Few Good Men
by Costin, Attorney

I've been a licensed attorney for a few years. After taking the bar exam, I clerked for a federal judge for a one-year term. Since my clerkship ended at the end of last year, I've had a very difficult time finding another position.

The prestige of my clerkship was supposed to guarantee me a great job. However, the status of the current economy and the low demand for entry-level attorneys has made my career transition very difficult.

I've attempted to use my law school's career services office, and I've used my own personal network. So far, nothing has panned out. I continue to search often and have even looked outside of the legal profession. Unfortunately, those outside the legal profession view me as overqualified.

I would encourage those in similar situations to take this time to reassess their career paths and attempt to transfer their skills from their previous positions into new career options. I would also encourage those in transition to attempt to remain positive. But trust me, I totally understand that this is often much easier said than done.

and refresh your mind for when you return to the grueling nine-to-five world back home.

Total Recall

- If you've been laid off or fired, evaluate what happened that got you to this point. Learn from the experience to further develop yourself and your professional aspirations.

- While unemployed, don't fall into unproductive routines. TV is not your friend. Treat looking for a new job as a full-time job.

- Stay organized and keep detailed files during your job search. Sending two resumes to the same company doesn't increase your chances of being interviewed.

- Use any time away from work to strengthen your skill set and to build your experiences. Are there opportunities for school, professional development, internships, volunteering, or working abroad? Don't be afraid to take some risks.

Floatation Devices

(or other helpful resources
you've got to check out)

Helpful Online Resources

Jobs, Networking, and Industry Information

www.monster.com

www.hotjobs.com

www.careerbuilder.com

www.directemployers.com

www.salary.com

www.wetfeet.com

www.craigslist.org

Personal Finance

www.fool.com

www.moneycentral.com

www.bankrate.com

www.smartmoney.com

www.finance.yahoo.com

www.insure.com

Saving Dough When Traveling

www.hotwire.com   www.expedia.com
www.priceline.com   www.hotels.com
www.orbitz.com   www.amtrak.com
www.travelocity.com

Good Clean Fun and Distraction

www.theonion.com   www.dilbert.com
www.thesmokinggun.com   www.doonesbury.com

Helpful Books

Figuring Out a Career Path

What Color Is Your Parachute? 2004: A Practical Manual for Job-Hunters & Career-Changers, by Richard Nelson Bolles. Ten Speed Press, 2003.

Finding a Career that Works for You: A Step-by-Step Guide to Choosing a Career and Finding a Job, by Wilma Fellman. Independent Publishers Group, 2000.

Finding the Career that Fits You: The Companion Workbook to Your Career in Changing Times, by Larry Burkett and Lee Ellis. Moody Publishers, 1998.

Cool Careers for Dummies, by Marty Nemko. For Dummies, 2001.

Finding Your Perfect Work: The New Career Guide to Making a Living, Creating a Life, by Paul and Sarah Edwards. J. P. Tarcher, 2003.

The Money Is the Gravy: Finding the Career that Nourishes You, by John Clark. Warner Books, 2003.

Coming Alive from Nine to Five: A Career Search Handbook, by Betty Neville Michelozzi. McGraw-Hill Humanities/Social Sciences/Languages, 2003.

Overall Job Search

I Don't Know What I Want, but I Know It's Not This: A Step-By-Step Guide to Finding Gratifying Work, by Julie Jansen. Penguin USA, 2003.

Finding a Job You Can Love, by Ralph Mattson and Arthur Miller. P & R Press, 1999.

Job Hunting for Dummies, by Max Messmer. For Dummies, 1999.

10 Insider Secrets to Job Hunting Success! Everything You Need to Get the Job You Want in 24 Hours-Or Less! by Todd Bermont. Career Press, 2004.

Job Hunter's Sourcebook: Where to Find Employment Leads and Other Job Search Resources, by Kathleen Maki Potts. Gale Group, 2002.

Don't Send a Resume: And Other Contrarian Rules to Help Land a Great Job, by Jeffrey Fox. Hyperion, 2004.

Get a Job in 30 Days or Less: A Realistic Action Plan for Finding the Right Job Fast, by Matthew and Nanette Deluca. McGraw-Hill Trade, 1999.

College Grad Job Hunter: Insider Techniques and Tactics for Finding a Top-Paying Entry Level Job, by Brian Krueger. Adams Media Corporation, 2003.

Your Job Search Partner: A 10-Day, Step-by-Step, Opportunity-Producing Job Search Guide, by Cheryl Cage. Cage Consulting, Inc., 2002.

Job Search Secrets, by Donald Lussier. McGraw-Hill/Contemporary Books, 1998.

Winning the Job Game: The New Rules for Finding and Keeping the Job You Want, by Carol Kleiman. John Wiley & Sons, 2002.

Jobsmarts for Twentysomethings, by Bradley Richardson. Vintage Books, 1995.

12 Simple Secrets of Happiness at Work: Finding Fulfillment, Reaping Rewards, by Glenn Van Ekeren. Prentice Hall Press, 2001.

Gender and Ethnicity

The Smart Woman's Guide to Interviewing and Salary Negotiation, by Julie Adair King. Career Press, 1995.

Women for Hire: The Ultimate Guide to Getting a Job, by Tory Johnson. Perigee, 2002.

Hardball for Women: Winning at the Game of Business, by Pat Heim and Susan Golant. Plume, 1993.

Peterson's the Minority Career Guide: What African Americans, Hispanics, and Asian Americans Must Know to Succeed in Corporate America, by Michael Kastre. Peterson's Guides, 1993.

The Colorblind Career: What Every African American, Hispanic American and Asian American Needs to Succeed in Today's Tough Job Market, by Ollie Stevenson. Peterson's Guides, 1997.

Success Runs in Our Race: The Complete Guide to Effective Networking in the Black Community, by George Fraser. Amistad Press, 2004.

Best Careers for Bilingual Latinos, by Graciela Kenig. McGraw-Hill/Contemporary Books, 1998.

Networking

The Perfect Pitch: How to Sell Yourself for Today's Job Market, by David Andrusia. DIANE Publishing Co., 1997.

Practical Networking: How to Give and Get Help with Jobs, by Edward Flippen. 1stBooks Library, 2003.

High-Impact Telephone Networking for Job Hunters, by Howard Armstrong. Adams Media Corporation, 1992.

Power Networking: Using the Contacts You Don't Even Know You Have to Succeed in the Job You Want, by Marc Kramer. McGraw-Hill, 1997.

A Foot in the Door: Networking Your Way into the Hidden Job Market, by Katharine Hansen. Ten Speed Press, 2000.

The Networking Survival Guide: Get the Success You Want by Tapping into the People You Know, by Diane C. Darling. McGraw-Hill Trade, 2003.

Electronic Resumes & Online Networking, by Rebecca Smith. Career Press, 2000.

Dynamite Networking for Dynamite Jobs: 101 Interpersonal, Telephone and Electronic Techniques for Getting Job Leads, Interviews and Offers, by Ronald Krannich and Caryl Rae Krannich. Impact Publications, 1996.

Power Networking: 55 Secrets for Personal & Professional Success, by Donna Fisher. Bard Press, 1992.

Résumes and Cover Letters

Cover Letters that Knock 'Em Dead, by Martin John Yate. Adams Media Corporation, 2002.

Cover Letters for Dummies, by Joyce Lain Kennedy. For Dummies, 2000.

Dynamic Cover Letters for New Graduates, by Katharine Hansen. Ten Speed Press, 1998.

The Edge Resume and Job Search Strategy, by Bill Corbin. Jist Works, 2000.

200 Letters for Job Hunters, by William Frank. Ten Speed Press, 1993.

Interviewing

Programming Interviews Exposed: Secrets to Landing Your Next Job, by John Mongan and Noah Suojanen. John Wiley & Sons, 2000.

Haldane's Best Answers to Tough Interview Questions, by Bernard Haldane. Impact Publications, 2000.

Killer Interviews, by Frederick and Barbara Ball. McGraw-Hill Trade, 1996.

201 Best Questions to Ask on Your Interview, by John Kador. McGraw-Hill Trade, 2002.

Interview Strategies that Will Get You the Job You Want, by Andrea Kay. Betterway Publications, 1996.

The Interview Kit, by Richard Beatty. John Wiley & Sons, 2000.

Job Interviews for Dummies, by Joyce Lain Kennedy. For Dummies, 2000.

Best Answers to the 201 Most Frequently Asked Interview Questions, by Matthew Deluca. McGraw-Hill Trade, 1996.

101 Great Answers to the Toughest Interview Questions, by Ronald Fry. Career Press, 4th edition, 2000.

Ask the Headhunter: Reinventing the Interview to Win the Job, by Nick Corcodilos. Plume, 1997.

The 250 Job Interview Questions You'll Most Likely Be Asked, by Peter Veruki and Peter Venki. Adams Media Corporation, 1999.

Interview Power: Selling Yourself Face to Face, by Tom Washington. Mount Vernon Press, 2000.

The Interview Rehearsal Book, by Deb Gottesman. Penguin Putnam Inc., 1999.

Nail the Job Interview! 101 Dynamite Answers to Interview Questions, by Caryl Rae Krannich. Impact Publications, 2003.

International Jobs

International Job Finder: Where the Jobs Are Worldwide, by Daniel Lauber. Planning Communications, 2002.

The Directory of Websites for International Jobs: The Click and Easy Guide, by Ronald and Caryl Rae Krannich. Impact Publications, 2002.

The Global Citizen: A Guide to Creating an International Life and Career, by Elizabeth Kruempelmann. Ten Speed Press, 2002.

Work Worldwide: International Career Strategies for the Adventurous Job Seeker, by Nancy Mueller. Avalon Travel Publishing, 2000.

How to Get a Job in Europe, by Cheryl Matherly and Robert Sanborn. Planning Communications, 5th edition, 2003.

International Jobs: Where They Are and How to Get Them, by Nina Segal and Eric Kocher. Perseus Publishing, 6th edition, 2003.

Personal Finances

Get a Financial Life: Personal Finance in Your Twenties and Thirties, by Beth Kobliner. Fireside, 2000.

The Green Magazine Guide to Personal Finance: A No B.S. Book for Your Twenties and Thirties, by Ken Kurson. Main Street Books, 1998.

Personal Finance for Dummies, by Eric Tyson. For Dummies, 4th edition, 2003.

Debt Free by 30: Practical Advice for Young, Broke, & Upwardly Mobile, by Jason Anthony and Karl Cluck. Plume, 2001.

Please Send Money: A Financial Survival Guide for Young Adults on Their Own, by Dara Duguay. Sourcebooks Trade, 2001.

Living on Your Own

So You Want to Move Out? A Guide to Living on Your Own, by Rik Feeney. Richardson Publishing, 1994.

The Most Important Things You'll Need to Know Before You Start Living Life on Your Own, by John Gerger. Writers Club Press, 2002.

Career Changes

Switching Careers: Career Changers Tell How and Why They Did It: Learn How You Can Too, by Robert Otterbourg. Kiplinger Books, 2001.

The Harvard Business School Guide to Finding Your Next Job, by Robert Gardella. Harvard Business School Press, 2000.

Changing Careers for Dummies, by Carol McClelland. For Dummies, 2001.

The Pathfinder: How to Choose or Change Your Career for a Lifetime of Satisfaction and Success, by Nicholas Lore. Fireside, 1998.

From Here . . . to There: A Self-Paced Program for Transition in Employment, by Lawrence Stuenkel. Facts on Demand Press, 2002.

The Complete Idiot's Guide to Reinventing Yourself, by Jeffrey Davidson. Alpha Books, 2001.

What to Do When Laid Off, Fired, or Having Quit

Fired, Laid Off, Out of a Job: A Manual for Understanding, Coping, and Surviving, by Byron Simerson. Praeger Publishing, 2003.

Getting Fired: What to Do if You're Fired, Downsized, Laid Off, Restructured, Discharged, Terminated, or Forced to Resign, by Steven Mitchell Sack. Warner Books, 1999.

Career Comeback: 8 Steps for Getting Back on Your Feet When You're Fired, Laid Off, or Your Business Venture Has Failed—And Finding More Job Satisfaction than Ever, by Bradley Richardson. Broadway Books, 2004.

When You Lose Your Job: Laid Off, Fired, Early Retired, Relocated, Demoted, Unchallenged, by Cliff Hakim. Berrett-Koehler Publishing, 1993.

The Final Word

Well, after reading this book you should have your dream job in your dream city, doing what you've always dreamed of doing and making more money than you ever imagined.

Maybe not. But that's not really the point. As much advice as we and the hundreds of recent grads and professionals can share, the real honest truth is that most of your questions and qualms regarding your interests, the working world, your job track, and your career will be answered and quelled once you actually jump headfirst into the working world. So if you don't know exactly what job you'd like or you're not sure that you like your job as much as you should, don't sweat it. Learn from your experiences, keep an open mind, and give yourself a chance to get to a place where you're happy more often than you're not.

We wish you extraordinary success out there and hope that you found something in this book that's going to make your career journey easier, more exciting, more fun, or a bit more fulfilling.

With warm regards,
Ben, Ari, and Rachel

To learn more about Students Helping Students® books, read samples and student-written articles, share your own experiences with other students, suggest a topic, or ask questions, visit us at www.StudentsHelpingStudents.com!

We're always looking for fresh minds and new ideas!

Index

Students Helping Students™
Get the whole series of guides written *for* students *by* students.